T4-AQM-370

ALSO BY CAROL CASSELL

SWEPT AWAY

STRAIGHT FROM THE HEART

HOW TO TALK TO YOUR TEENAGERS ABOUT LOVE AND SEX

CAROL CASSELL, PH.D.

A FIRESIDE BOOK
PUBLISHED BY SIMON & SCHUSTER INC.
NEW YORK LONDON TORONTO SYDNEY TOKYO

First Fireside Edition, 1988
Published by Simon & Schuster Inc.
Simon & Schuster Building
Rockefeller Center
1230 Avenue of the Americas
New York, New York 10020

Manufactured in the United States of America
10 9 8 7 6 5 4 3 2
10 9 8 7 6 5 4 3 2 1 Pbk.

Library of Congress Cataloging in Publication Data

Cassell, Carol, date.
Straight from the heart.

Bibliography: p.
1. Sex instructions for youth. 2. Parenting.
3. Love. I. Title. [DNLM: 1. Adolescent Psychology—popular works. 2. Communication—popular works. 3. Love—popular works. 4. Parent-Child Relations—popular works. 5. Sex—popular works. WS 462 C344s]
HQ57.C37 1987 649'.65 86-29657

ISBN 0-671-60521-6
ISBN 0-671-66198-1 Pbk.

The author gratefully acknowledges permission from the following sources to quote material in the text:

Talking with Your Teenager: A Book for Parents by Ruth Bell and Leni Zeiger Wildflower, copyright © 1983, Random House, Inc. By permission of the publisher.

"Expectations, Not Sexual Development, Influence Adolescent Dating Behavior" by Sanford M. Dornbusch, *Sexuality Today*, June 1981, copyright © 1981. By permission of the author.

"The Turmoil of Teenage Sexuality" by Ellen Goodman, *MS.*, July 1983, copyright © 1983. By permission of the author.

Sex Education Begins at Home by Howard and Martha Lewis, copyright © 1983, Appleton-Century-Crofts. By permission of the publisher.

"Survey: Adolescent Dating" commentary by Anthony Pietropinto M.D., from *Medical Aspects of Human Sexuality*, December 1984, copyright © 1984, Hospital Publications, Inc. By permission of the publisher.

The Patient Patients' Book by Planned Parenthood of Tompkins County, © 1980. By permission.

ACKNOWLEDGMENTS

My appreciation to all the young people who shared their concerns, stresses, and successes and helped me see through their eyes the challenge of coming-of-age in today's world. A special thanks to those in Appleton and Oshkosh, Wisconsin; Albuquerque (particularly the students at Manzano High School) and Santa Fe, New Mexico; Stillwater, Oklahoma; Gettysburg, Pennsylvania; Hollins College, Roanoke, Virginia; and, Lubbock, Texas.

To the teachers and counselors who made invaluable contributions, my gratitude, especially Paulette Allen, Debbie Maki, and Carol Heid (who gets a double gold star).

For their critical review of the manuscript, I thank Sue Steed, John and Glo Cantwell, Brett Barker, and Lydia Neumann. Special appreciation to Elizabeth Canfield for her careful editing and helpful suggestions. And to Kay Scott, my friend and sounding board, for her insightful contributions to each draft.

I owe a debt of gratitude to Jonathan Dolger, my literary

agent, for his unerring ability to sift the chaff from the wheat. And to Patricia Soliman, my outstanding editor, for her encouragement, and whose critical eye and perspective made this a better book. Further thanks to Cheryl Weinstein for being so helpful, and Debra Makay for her superb copyediting.

To my parents, Dorothy and Al Miller, my special thanks for shepherding me through my turbulent teenage years in such good humor. And to my three terrific brothers, who gave me the priceless experience of hearing the boys' side of things while growing up: Tom, for making me laugh; John, for being such a champ; and Phil, for being such a good pal and listening to my first "sex education" lecture.

To my husband and friend, Bob, my loving appreciation for his unfaltering patience, support, and optimistic outlook on life that helps to remind me that there's bound to be a pony somewhere.

For my wonderful children,
Don, Alisa, John, Michael,
and my stepdaughters, Emily and Lisa.
And for grandson Justin, the family's future teenager.

CONTENTS

AUTHOR'S NOTE

Throughout this book, when I refer to your children, teens, or adolescents, I'm not assuming most families have more than one child, I simply prefer to use the unisex pronoun "they" or "them" instead of the generic "he." Occasionally, I do the same (even though it means a disagreement of subject and pronoun) when I refer to "your teen" and continue the sentence with "they" to avoid the awkwardness of too many he/she, his/her constructions. One of my fondest hopes is to see the acceptance of unisex language in this decade. It's time.

PREFACE

THIS BOOK IS FOR PARENTS WHO find themselves reeling backward, and feeling slightly chagrined, at their jittery-skittery knee-jerk reaction to their teenagers' budding, or obviously blooming, interest in the opposite sex. Many of you sexually came of age, chronologically or emotionally, in the heady days of the sexual revolution. You want to avoid the pitfalls of tracking girls onto the well-worn guilt and anxiety Good Girl/Bad Girl path of sexuality. And you don't applaud traditional double-standard behavior for boys—having sex to rack up points on a macho scorecard. On the one hand you want your son or daughter to feel comfortable about sexuality; on the other hand you don't want to see them becoming involved with sex too soon. But it's not as easy to get these ideas across as you thought it would be.

As I travel around the country lecturing and conducting seminars about sexuality it has become overwhelmingly evident that a brave new generation of parents—the survivors of the sexual revolution—is in a unique quandary as to how to deal with the topics of sex, love, and contraception with their teens or soon-to-be teens. Parents, especially those who once spearheaded life-styles of sexual liberation, wonder if their kids can handle, or if they will be hurt by, the kind of sexual freedom that seems to exist today. Yet, they aren't hankering to return to the stereotypical sexual roles and rules of their parents' generation.

And so this book. It is a practical guide for parents, married or single, on how to help a son or daughter become a sane and sensible sexual person, without the sexual hang-ups of the past, but with an appreciation of the responsibilities involved in having sexual choices.

My advice is based upon a mixture of anecdotes, theory, and research, but mostly upon my experience: personal, as a parent of six (four of my own and two step) kids, and professional, working for years in the field of human sexuality. Too often I've seen adults focus on teenage sex and pregnancy without paying much attention to the most compelling part of young life: the bittersweetness of love. I know that's a big oversight. And so, I've put an emphasis on giving you real insight into how teens feel about falling in love, trying to develop relationships, and mending a broken heart. Also highlighted is the role love plays as the inspiration and the driving force behind sexual desires.

My thinking has been shaped by the experiences and opinions of the uncountable number of young people I've had the privilege to talk with. I've directly quoted many of their concerns and views. I know hearing their voices will key you in on what may be going on underneath the preppy to punk exterior of your son or daughter.

What *you* think about sexuality is the benchmark of your communications with your teen. Thus, there is an opportunity here for you to sort out your *own* feelings and clarify your ethical values about sexuality: a personal sexual inventory exercise.

You'll find tips on how to have a candid conversation with your teen: when to initiate a discussion and when to wait until asked. And how to identify where they are on the adolescent emotional and sexual development continuum so you can be prepared to deal with their needs for information and tender loving care. Then, there are chapters covering those topics teenage life revolves around: love, sex, relationships, and surviving a broken heart (the sine qua non of teen romance). Other chapters discuss how to help them understand homosexuality, contraception, pregnancy, and sexually transmitted diseases.

To make it easy for you to get a handle on those critical issues, most of the chapters follow a pattern:

1. A perspective on the topic along with guidelines on how to discuss it with your teen.
2. A summary of the factual information.

Then, turn to the back of the book where you'll find some special help: *Practice Sessions*. I'll share with you many of the most commonly asked questions I've had from teens: some asked out loud; some which they handed me written out on cards because they were too shy, or didn't want to be singled out in a crowd. These will provide you with the "inside track" on what is on young people's minds and what you need to talk to your teen about. To lend a hand to your efforts, I've provided you with a sample of how I typically respond to these questions.

Also, there are a few case studies to give you an opportunity to think through how you would react and what advice you would give, if you were on the spot. These "what ifs" are based upon real-life situations teens have described to me. Others are from the "what should I do/have done" discussions I've had with parents in my workshops. And here again, you can compare and contrast a sample of my advice with your own.

Now I'm not trying to put words into your mouth. Pick and choose what makes sense to you, say what *you* want to, and say it in your way, in your own words.

I'm not implying that enlightening your teens about the facts of life, and guiding them through their intoxicating affairs of the heart, is a snap. It isn't. But it's not all that difficult either. After all, every one of us is here in this world because of sex. And when it comes to knowing about love, well, we didn't give up being a lover when we became a parent.

Note:

While this book is primarily for parents, it should be helpful for any adult—aunt, uncle, older sister or brother, grandmother or grandfather, friend—who cares about a young person and hopes to guide them into having healthy and responsible attitudes toward sexuality.

CHAPTER ONE

THE WAY IT IS

IT WAS NEAR THE VERY END of the "Donahue" show, where I was appearing on a book tour, when a woman—tall, attractive, late-thirtyish—stood up and asked me: "I have a 20-year-old son. How do I tell him, without sounding archaic and sounding the way I was brought up, 'Respect the girls'? We all want to be liberated. Great. But how do you tell your daughter, 'Well, Mother thought it was all right for her, but really, honey, I don't want you doing this'? How do you keep a 13- or 14- or 15-year-old girl from sleeping around? Yet acknowledge that by, say, age 28, she'll have had several sexual partners. How can she be normal?"

"First of all," I told her, "we have to talk about sexual chemistry and biology, the wonderful drive we all feel—and it's real—and tell our sons that women have as much right to express these feelings as men do. Then, we need to talk about sexual ethics. Not virginity and chastity; we have to use new words that make more sense. Talk about sexual exploitation, manipulation, and honesty. We can talk to teenagers, both boys and girls, about postponing sex until they are at a time of their life when they can handle the consequences, physical and emotional." I wanted to say more, but there was no time; the show quickly moved on, and, poof, it was over. I went away feeling frustrated—I had hardly scratched the surface.

But that brief dialogue spurred me on to write this book, because it echoed what so many other parents I've talked with have on their minds.

As Diana, a single mother of a 13-year-old daughter, put it: "I was pretty casual about sex when I was in college. I slowed down when I graduated because I didn't need to prove I was liberated anymore. I began to sort out what was really a reaction to the pressure about having sex because it was expected, and what I wanted for myself. I hope my daughter won't have to make the same mistakes. She's always been so sensible, but lately she's getting boy-crazy. I worry that sex can't be far off. But how do you get the idea across that sex is great but you have to use discretion without sounding like a fan of Laverne and Shirley's great holdout schemes?"

It isn't only the parents of daughters who find themselves stuttering when it comes to talking about sexual relationships. Jack, the father of three teenage sons, talks about wanting to raise them, "not in the old macho mold": "I want each of them to understand that putting pressure on a woman to have sex isn't fair or moral. I did my share of that and feel really bad about how I was so callous. I envisioned myself having heart-to-heart, father-to-son talks with each of them about women, sex, and 'becoming a man,' but so far our little talks have been few and far between. Any mention of sex deteriorates into the three of them trading gross jokes. Or I get the 'Ahhh, Dad' routine. It's ironic how hard it is for me to broach the topic of sex —I earn my living by conducting management seminars and I'm sure no one would believe I can be tongue-tied about anything! But damn it I am."

Like Diana and Jack, when it comes to discussing the exhilarating feelings of love and the intriguing facts of sex with their son or daughter, almost all parents, myself included, vacillate between an easy acceptance of their adolescent's sexual stirrings and downright alarm that it's happening now. Their transition from girl to woman, boy to man, sneaks up on us.

But as a parent of rapidly maturing children, you know you need to say *something*. You don't want your teenage son or daughter fumbling their way through a maze of confusion about the pleasure and pain of falling in and out of love, and suffering the consequences of being naive about sex. But you get stuck somewhere between your good intentions and a waffling uncertainty about exactly what to say and when to say it.

THE "TALK"

Take heart. You don't have to be an expert equipped with flip charts and diagrams to communicate about love and sex. It's perfectly all right to admit you don't have a slick set of answers to everything, or that you feel at sea and uncomfortable.

You may have the impression that sometime in the near future the perfect setting and time will arise for you to have that "talk" with your teen. Don't count on it.

First of all, kids ask questions, or show an interest in discussing sex, when we least expect it: on their way out of the door to school, when we are trying to get ourselves together to go to work, or ten minutes before eight people are coming over to dinner. Well, you get the picture.

All of this means you can forget about the ideal moment

and place for a "talk." You could never hope to cover all of the important things to say about the topic in one sitting anyway—it would last longer than a Labor Day telethon. The best way to give your teen (or soon-to-be teen) information about sexuality is slowly, over time, through informal and spontaneous conversations.

You don't have to wait for them to bring up something about love and sex. Your son or daughter may not have the nerve to bring up whatever is on their mind, or they may be a little foggy about what it is they want to ask you. Sometimes they may ask a question in such a vague way that you'll miss your cue. So, be prepared to take the initiative. But before you clear your throat, read on.

THE SEXUAL REVOLUTION AND TEENS

The sexual revolution that began on college campuses in the sixties has filtered down to high schools and junior high schools. A cold harsh reality is that peer pressure—the ephemeral disease of teenagehood—is as alive and well as it ever was, and it is a lot more persuasive than we are. Today, teens face a kind of reverse peer pressure from the fifties—it is more in tune with the sixties and seventies—the pressure to lose, rather than keep, one's virginity. And this pressure provides, for a lot of teens, the push to take the sexual plunge. The time between first kiss and intercourse is incredibly fast: About 80 percent of boys and 70 percent of girls report having sex while still in their teens. By age 15, one girl in five has had sex; by age 17, half of all girls. Even among teens who have not yet experienced intercourse, there is a stated willingness to do so, providing they feel "ready" and meet the "right" person.

That's the way it is. It matters not that today's sexual mores delight or disgust you. You need to learn how teens deal with all of this to get a grip on the reality of teenage sexuality, relationships, and the possibility of teen pregnancy. Better to know than to be a member of the parental head-in-the-sand club.

In spite of teenage sexual emancipation, and the fact that they may be a little more savvy about fallopian tubes than you might have been, there are no guarantees they will choose wisely when faced with decisions about contraception and safe sex. Take, for instance, the incredible rate of teenage pregnancies—over one million teenage girls, one out of ten, get pregnant each year. And sexually transmitted diseases are rampant among teens—teens contract about 25 percent of all of the one million gonorrhea cases every year. For all the lip service paid to sexual sophistication, teens' sexual maturity runs breathlessly ahead of their emotional development.

Sex and bubble gum are the signs of the times. It's enough to prematurely gray the hair of even the most liberal-minded parent.

OWNING UP

I know the issue of what the sexual revolution has wrought is complex, and some of the fallout needs revamping. However, before we get sidetracked into thinking we ought to retreat into thc safety of the restrictive days of yesteryear, let's own up to a critical truth. Putting the confusion about how young people deal with sexual freedom aside, would you really want to turn the clock back to chastity until marriage? Most people, with good reason, believe things are better than they were, say, in the pre–sexual revolution days. Women are less available for exploitation, and most men simply no longer feel honor bound to prove, or publicize, their manhood by pursuing close encounters of the desperate kind.

Actually, we are living in a sexual transition era. Our

notions are a potpourri: some ideas left over from the fifties, others evolving from a pinch of this and a pinch of that from the sixties and seventies. No wonder we can feel one way intellectually, and another way emotionally, about our kid's sexuality.

Still, I've seen too many parents who aren't advocates of "traditional" sexual mores hesitate to admit it to their teens. They are maddeningly elusive about their beliefs.

We need to keep our concerns about teenage sexuality in perspective: The benefits of sexual emancipation—more choice for everyone and a healthier sense of one's own sexuality—far outweigh its shortcomings. So don't be shy about expressing a positive and contemporary point of view. Your teen is the better for it: Healthy and positive attitudes about sex are part and parcel of self-esteem and the ability to develop satisfying relationships.

SILENCE ISN'T GOLDEN

Your teen hungers for the chance to have a "warts and all" conversation with you. They want you to tell them what you think, *really* think, about falling in love, being in a close relationship, and where sex fits into the scheme of things.

Without anything having been said to them directly, they have already picked up bits and pieces of information about your attitudes toward these subjects. They eavesdrop on conversations, size up reactions to TV, gossip, and the news. They know more than you think about your feelings about premarital sex, extramarital sex, babies born out of wedlock, homosexuality, living together, marriage, and every other shading of relationships. But because they hear only fragments of your conversations they usually don't perceive the total content or context of your opinions, which means they have received a muddled mix of messages—ranging from acceptance to disapproval of any number of behaviors or values about sexuality. They aren't always very clear about what exactly it is that you think, or what you expect of them. You need to set the record straight.

THE SORTING OUT: A PERSONAL INVENTORY

You can begin by sifting out from the sexual debris of the last three decades what you *really* think about sex, passion, love, and all the rest of those marvelously wacky parts of our lives. Now that's no mean feat. But to set up a two-way dialogue with our kids, we have to own up to our own views and values about sexual behavior and responsibility before we can discuss theirs.

This means taking the time *right now* for a personal sexual inventory. Get a pad of blank paper, a pen or pencil, and write out your responses. These short exercises are designed to help you examine your own attitudes and what influenced your thinking about sexuality. If you are part of a couple, each of you can do this separately, and then share and discuss your responses.

A PERSONAL INVENTORY

PART 1: SEXUAL INITIATION

"When I first became aware that men and women had sexual intercourse, I thought ________________."

"When I was in high school, and I looked in the mirror, I saw ________________."

"As I began to develop, I was ________________."

"My memories of having my first few periods (or wet dreams) are ________________."

"The first time I fell in love, I thought it was ________."
"The first time I had sex I ________."
"When I heard about 'getting pregnant' I was ________."
"When I heard about birth control I was ________."
"The message I heard the most about love, sex, and/or marriage from my parents was ________."
"When my first love broke up with me, I felt ________."
"What I learned about sex from my religion was ________."
"Being 'with it' in my high school meant ________."
"Growing up I heard that Good Girls were ________."
"Growing up I heard that Bad Girls were ________."
"I thought, when it came to sex, guys (girls) were ________."
"Compared to the other guys (girls) I was ________."
"When I was a teen my idea of being an adult was ________."
"I wish my mother/father had told me ________."

PART TWO: DEFINING WORDS AND PHRASES

On a separate piece of paper, briefly define the following words or phrases—not what the dictionary says, but what they mean to you:

brief encounter
promiscuity
premarital sex
extramarital sex
abortion
virgin
intimacy
love
slut
stud
commitment
masculinity
femininity
marriage
living together
unwed mother
teenage sex
making love
having sex
petting
sexual freedom
homosexuality
going steady
responsible sex
safe sex

Go back and read all of your responses and definitions. Any surprises? Any "not sures"?

Then, put the personal inventory away in a place from which you can retrieve it after you have read this book. When you take it back out, read it over. Any additions? Deletions? Make any necessary changes.

Next, consider all of the factors involved—other people's influences and your own experience—that have shaped your sexual attitudes and behavior. After you've mulled all of this over, try to clarify *your* philosophy about sexuality and write it down. Discuss your thoughts with your partner or friends and listen to their points of view.

Then, all by yourself, commit to paper what is the *essential* message you want to get across to your teen about love, sex, conception, contraception, intimacy, and male-female relationships.

There is no blueprint, no software program that will put together some perfectly honed truth—your values, your experience, your hopes and dreams for them are what's important. If, as a couple, you and your partner don't agree on everything, fine: Respect these differences but decide how you will communicate to your teen *why* you each feel the way you do.

CHAPTER TWO

EASING INTO A DISCUSSION

THAT OLD NUGGET—THE GENERATION gap—is often fingered as the reason why parents and teens don't always see eye-to-eye. But that's not the whole story. While each generation does have its own world view, the biggest barrier is the same as it is for all human relationships: failure to talk, failure to listen, and failure to make enough of an effort to understand the other person's point of view.

Don't be dismayed if, when you attempt to initiate a dialogue with your teen, he or she is a bit resistant or evasive. They are eager and not so eager to talk to you—all at the same time. For many teens, sex is a topic to be avoided when in the presence of adults, maybe you included, because they have learned it touches off a lot of adult embarrassment or anxiety. They may be uncertain whether you really do want to talk about sex openly.

Many teens say they are leery about disclosing their sexual curiosity because it might "set their parents off." They feel it's safer all around to shield their parents from the actual facts of life today. As one teenager said, "My mother would have a stroke if she knew how much sex my friends have. She wouldn't let me hang out with them, and I wouldn't have any friends." Craig, a 17-year-old, told me, "The parent has to make the first move. If you bring something up they go on and on. You are in for one big lecture. It's hard to talk to your parents about what goes on at parties and stuff. So I tell them only what I think won't freak them out. But I'd rather be straight with them."

Compounding the problem, and adding to their apprehension about your reactions, is their own uneasiness with their changing sexual selves. They worry that their sexual feelings are abnormal, or bizarre. And they have a lot of coping to do: getting teased by their school chums about how their body looks, trying to be part of the bevy of dirty jokes, passing muster in the locker room, dealing with constant innuendos about their sexual experiences (or lack thereof).

Sometimes they cover up their embarrassment by putting on an air of indifference or superiority, or acting bored or preoccupied, when you try to talk to them. Teens are the absolute champs of "cutting a person off" by their skillful application of a maddeningly disdainful look of cool amusement at our fumbling attempts to communicate. Try to remember that being overeager and undereager, overwhelmed and underwhelmed, is all a part of their sexual growing up.

It's hard to recall how important it was to us when *we* were teens to march in perfect precision to the same drumbeat as everyone else our age. But it was to us, and it is to them. Nobody craves popularity and acceptance and hates being branded a freak more than teens. And navigating the halls of high school is both as exhilarating and miserable as it has always been, for all of us.

Keep the big picture in mind as your guide, which is to

help them to take pleasure in their developing sexuality, have them understand their changing bodies, and help them cope with their emotional peaks and valleys. And when you think about it, helping a young person to cope with the sexual side of growing up has to be one of the sweetest and most privileged parts of being a parent.

Your willingness to be honest and direct will go a long way. Keep letting them know you care, you love them, and you believe in them, and you will eventually connect.

DISCUSSION TIPS

With all of this in mind, here are some ways to broach the subject of sexuality with your teen, and some hints about how to handle the situation once the ice has been broken.

Seize the Moment

Conversations flow a lot easier when they are not "programmed." Driving somewhere, doing a job together, or loafing around reading the Sunday newspaper are perfect times for the natural give-and-take that takes the edge off an "on-the-spot" feeling—yours or theirs. Watching TV can open up any number of opportunities to make a comment and ask for their opinion: Many TV offerings, from dramas to comedies, feature sexual situations. Soap operas have unlimited possibilities. And there are always those documentaries. Read the words to some popular music (popular with kids, that is) on record albums (the words are difficult for those over 21 to hear)—the lyrics are an education in themselves, and are a useful way to tune into the teen culture. When they are listening to music, discuss the messages songs convey about love, passion, stereotypes, sexual violence, and more.

BE ALERT TO "TEACHABLE MOMENTS"

Stay tuned-in to how your teen's body is changing. Breasts bud. Underarm hair sprouts. Each of these physical changes is an opportunity to share with them some facts about sexual development. But never give in to the slightest urge to make a joke about it, or tease them. NEVER. It causes them great grief. Jan, 14, told me, "My dad told me I was going to give Dolly Parton some competition in a few years and I nearly *died.*"

Some easy openers could be, "You are really growing up. One of the experiences you may soon have, or already have had, is a 'wet dream.' Wet dreams are called nocturnal emissions because they usually happen in the middle of the night during a dream. This happens because . . ." You can then go into a few biological facts (see Chapter 3) with a lot of reassurance that all is "normal."

GET TO THE POINT

Answer what they really want to know. Don't barge in with a tedious explanation, and resist jumping to conclusions. If your daughter asks, "Are birth control pills dangerous?", don't leap to the assumption that she is taking them. Teens often ask questions about something they want to file away for future use. Just be as matter-of-fact as you can be. And don't labor under the delusion that you have to know the answer to everything. If you don't really feel sure about the facts, say so. Then offer to look it up—together, if you can. After all, you can't know everything. Science and social patterns have shattered old ideas, brought about new problems. For example, test-tube babies were in the realm of science fiction in our youth. And did you know that chlamydia is the nation's number 1 sexually transmitted disease?

It's always a good idea to get them their own book on teenage sexuality (see the list in the back of this book). Talk about it with them.

Honor Their Privacy

Teens are very touchy about their personal lives. Resist the notion to share something they have told you with your friends, no matter how cute. Teens hate the idea that what they do, or don't do, might be discussed behind their backs. Many tell me they would like to confide in one of their parents but they "don't trust them." "Right away my mom would blab to my father or her best friend," is what I've heard as a barrier to communication over and over again. Sorry, but that's the way a lot of teens really feel.

Let them know you will respect their confidence and safeguard their privacy—and stick to your word.

Go Beyond the Obvious, but with Caution

If you sense that behind a question lies a deeper concern, check it out. But proceed with caution. They resent anything even bordering on being intrusive, no matter how well intended. *Don't probe.* The slightest essence of parental pushiness turns a teenager into a clam. Let them know you are open to hearing what is on their mind. Say something like, "I'm glad you brought that up." Depending on how comfortable you, and they, are at the moment, you can add, "Is there something else you want to talk about?" Or, "Did I answer what you asked?"

Stop When Enough Is Enough

Don't force a heavy talk when a once-over-lightly is what is on your teen's mind, or you'll find your son or daughter digging in their heels. Watch for signals indicating they have had all they can handle: a glazed look, eyes that focus over your shoulder, the sound of footsteps as they flee from your presence. Don't get uptight. You are not a failure. Remember that you are in anxiety-prone territory. Let them know you do care about what they are doing without pushing for "letting-it-all-hang-out" intimacy. Some teens feel their parents are overly curious about their sex lives, that they press too hard for details about what happens on dates. Many teens view "sharing" feelings, or information about one's sex life, as inappropriate. For example, in psychologist Robert Sorenson's study, six out of ten teenagers said, "I don't talk to my parents about my sex life because it is a personal subject and my own business."

Stay available. Leave the door open.

DON'T POP A TRIAL BALLOON

To protect themselves from getting into any possible trouble, teens speak in indirect code, or send up a trial balloon to test our reactions. Usually they bring up something about a friend, or "someone" at school. How we react to their gossip gives them a clue as to how we might respond if they were in the same situation. Don't try to find out the "who" in these questions.

Allow the distancing factor to be an asset. Without your teen feeling they are on center stage, they will bring up sensitive subjects that might be too difficult for them to talk about directly. And, what better time to show empathy for the complexities and vulnerabilities of human relationships? You can reinforce the point that we all make mistakes, or do things we later regret. Maybe you had a "friend" once in the same spot?

DISCUSS, DON'T DICTATE

You can articulate high standards for behavior without denying your teen the right to their own feelings. Instead of making pronouncements and judgments, use low-key thought provokers: "What do you think are the consequences of being deeply involved with someone?" "Do you think sex is something everybody does or everybody talks about?" "Why are there so many 'dirty' jokes about sex?"

It can be an awesome task for teens to consider all sides of the question, but a conclusion reached through thinking things out, mulling pros and cons, is one that has lasting power. Your messages will have a better chance of being received if they aren't the old-style forced feeding of parental dictates.

Speak Out but Don't Expect Compliance

Don't waffle about the fact that you have a set of standards about sexual relationships because, along with a healthy acceptance about sexuality, you want to instill in your teen a set of responsible sexual values. Discuss how you have arrived at the values you have, and lay out what you think is appropriate. Essentially, you need to get across the message that you want them to benefit from your experience and observations.

Make clear that you recognize they are trying to find their own way and live their own life, but you want them to consider what you have to say. You don't have to take on the demeanor of a saintly, nonjudgmental person. As a grown-up, we've earned our stripes. It is ridiculous to allow our experiences and accumulated knowledge to be too lightly dismissed by our teens. Jennifer, the parent of a 13-year-old, tells of the time she was going toe-to-toe with her daughter in a dispute over the merit of going steady, when she stopped short and said, "Look, maybe I'm not 'with-it' by your standards, but I arrived at my values through a lot of thought and experience. If you decide that what I think isn't right for you, that's your decision. But don't just dismiss what I have to say without thinking about it." I couldn't have put it better myself. Only don't become so preoccupied with what you want to say that you miss what *they* have to say.

And don't get overly huffy when they poke holes in your values. Let's admit it: It's easy to listen to our teens' world view of life when they parrot our beliefs, but when they don't, it is frustrating. Explain to them that you believe in their right to have their own opinions. You aren't interested in "winning" an argument. You are open to new information. And acknowledge that you could change your mind about something in the future, and they might also. Remember, teens sometimes argue and disagree for the simple joy of rebelling and thumbing their nose at "the establishment." Thus, don't get drawn into a battle of wills. Simply exercise your right to express yourself, to be listened to courteously. And grant them the same. Repress any inclination to belittle their opinions, no matter how naive and fanciful their thinking seems. They are experimenting with new ideas, testing out your reactions, and testing theirs as well. Be a good sounding board.

Even if they aren't on the same wavelength with you, let them know that you can be counted on to help them cope with the vicissitudes of life. You are there to guide them into making the kinds of decisions that influence their lives in a positive way. Convey to them that that is what being a parent is all about. You may need to repeat it many times. Sometimes kids forget.

BE DISCREET ABOUT YOUR OWN SEX LIFE

I'm not convinced it's ever a good idea to go into full disclosure about your own sex life, even if you are *very* comfortable about your own sexuality and *very* sure your teen would somehow benefit from knowing. While few parents could discuss their personal carnal knowledge with any iota of comfort, a vast majority of teens don't even want to know about their parents' sexual biographies; it is too threatening to them. Maybe this discomfort is linked to the incest taboo, or it could be that it crosses a line we are not consciously aware of, yet one we know intuitively is better left uncrossed.

Most likely, it never occurs to your teen that you have a sex life anyway. When I try to get my university students to consider sexuality over the life cycle, they draw a blank. They are often embarrassed at the very idea, and mumble something to the effect that "if older people have sex, it's not often." Researcher Ollie Pocs found that all categories of youth find it difficult to think of their parents as being sexually active. He says, "In youth's perception, even parents in their forties have little if any sex life."

All around, I think it would be healthier if teens did understand that sexuality is an integral aspect of the human condition throughout life. Unfortunately, our collective cultural anxiety about sex makes it difficult for teens to be comfortable and accepting of adult (read "parent") sexuality.

SEX AND THE SINGLE PARENT

For a parent who is single, raising a teen and having a personal sexual life are difficult to balance. For married couples, their bedroom is their sanctuary and what happens behind closed doors is either mostly blocked out by their kids or ignored. But it's a great deal more complicated for a single parent. If you stay over at someone's home, or if they stay at yours (in your bedroom, that is), you are making a statement about having sex. You could pretend you are only platonic friends, but it's a fruitless ruse.

Now, I'm not advocating celibacy until your teen is out of the nest, or concealment—only the use of discretion. Why? You may be unwittingly setting up a role model your teenager is ill-equipped to handle. Lynn, a 13-year-old, says, "I hate it when my mom's latest boyfriend spends the night at our house. It's so embarrassing. I can't invite a friend to sleep over because I wouldn't know what to say if he shows up in the kitchen for breakfast. Sometimes I don't even know his name. And she has the nerve to lecture me about boys!"

Besides the role-model situation, you need to be aware of other reasons that make many teens uneasy about their single parent's sexual relationships. Some teens worry that their parent is being too casual about sex, and will get (or give them) a "bad reputation." As Jane, age 15, explains, "It looks terrible having all these different women coming and going out of our apartment at all hours of the night. I know our neighbors talk about it, and think our family is kinda sleazy."

Granted, they don't seem to give their single-again parent enough credit for having good judgment. Still, their concern about a parent's sexual liaisons is genuine. Teens are not without experience at seeing a parent suffer when a lover is thoughtless, or disappears from the scene without any notice. Many teens feel apprehensive about their parent's well-being, and worry that the parent may be falling "head over heels" and may take a hard lump if the affair ends badly. Others are concerned that their parent (usually the mother) is being, as teens put it, "used."

Teens want their parent to be able to mend the wounds of divorce, to be happy. They don't object to their parent trying to find someone to love again. It is the nomadic character of sexual relationships involving their single parent that seems to bother teens the most. Some teens wonder what will come of it all. As several have pointed out to me, the number of lovers they have seen come and go is "a whole lot."

MARRIED OR SINGLE

This doesn't mean, whether you are married or single, that you have to reinforce the myth that a parent is asexual. You don't have to hide the fact that you are a sexual person and you don't need to lie about it. Not at all. Just use discretion, not secrecy or phony smoke screens.

Exchanging signs of affection with your partner or mate —hugging, pats on the rear end, kissing with enthusiasm —signals to your teen that sexual feelings are natural, and a wonderful part of a relationship. Respond in a positive way if they ask "Do you have sex?" by casually saying something to the effect of "Sure," "Of course," or "Sometimes," or whatever sums up your situation.

CHAPTER THREE

TEENAGERS, AKA ADOLESCENTS

THIS CHAPTER IS MOSTLY a memory clicker for those who have mercifully forgotten what a friend wryly labeled "The most confusing era of my life but one somehow cheerfully touted by teachers and family as 'The Happiest Years of Your Life.' " Looking back, Lee Ranck, a counselor, describes what it was like for most of us: "We were awkward, unstable, impulsive, exuberant, depressed, vital, lazy, thoughtless, jealous, sensitive, a little bit loony, and at times awfully wise. We were growing, maturing, daydreaming, developing, testing, trying on, exploring, experimenting, experiencing new life. We had stumbled into a rolling barrel in an amusement fun house and were trying to stand up but we were flopping and flipping around . . . loving and hating, accepting and rebelling, groping toward the far end of that whirling experience." Ahhh, those were the days all right.

I remember groping very graphically. Going to "make-out" parties, playing hide-and-seek as an excuse to sneak away and kiss until my lips were numb. Progressing to parking on Lovers' Lookout and darkened rooms at parties where groping got more serious. All that kissing, fondling, hugging, whispering "I love you" (and meaning it)—the tingling feelings that made my cheeks a blotchy hot pink and my eyes overly bright.

I guess I enjoyed myself. I must have, at least once in a while. But mostly I recall being scared, worried about "going too far," insecure about "what he thought of me," and fearful of enjoying myself too much. I had a yellow angora sweater that drove my boyfriend (the love of my ninth-grade life) wild. He was addicted to its soft fluffy touch. By the time "The End" flashed on the screen of the drive-in theater, he looked a little like a baby chick—yellow down covered his navy blue letterman sweater, his white open-collared shirt, and his gray-flannel pants. All the way home, I would pick tiny fuzz balls off him while I tried to smooth out my wondrous sweater, glancing out the car window to wish upon a star that he really did love me and that we would be steadies forever (or at least until graduation).

Knowing that carnal experimentation (except for a friendly good-night kiss) was strictly forbidden made me feel embarrassed and ashamed that I wasn't what I seemed to be—the ultimate Good Girl coed. Going back into the school gym after a visit to the parking lot during the band's intermission at a dance was bad enough, but nothing could compare to having to go home after a "real" date. I would pray with all the zest of a repented sinner that my parents would already be in bed, or distracted watching TV, and therefore not witness my reentry into the house so they could grill me about "the kind of time I had." To this day, when I see a yellow angora sweater, I nearly break out in hives.

No matter how you remember your adolescence, I'll bet

that sexuality was at the center of your turmoil, just as it was mine. No wonder. Our bodies were doing strange and wonderful things, and our minds harbored tantalizing thoughts, fantasies, and desires. Whether or not we acted upon our desires, talked as though we had, or silently went off by ourselves behind a locked bathroom door to explore our mysterious body parts and touch ourselves in awe of how good it felt—none of us could completely ignore our emerging sexual feelings and desires.

LOOKING OVER YOUR SHOULDER

A way to understand what your child is experiencing, or will experience, is to recall your own adolescence. Looking back can make us smile, even chuckle out loud, as we mentally or physically flip through the pages of the photo albums of junior high and high school. However, reflecting about how we dealt with our changing bodies and emotions is not without some pain. Some of us bring along a lot, some of us just a little baggage from our adolescent years —fear, guilt, insecurity, prejudices (maybe even flinching at yellow sweaters).

We all walk around with some unresolved conflicts and scars and wounds suffered in the trauma of growing up. But somehow we managed to grow up, to enter the ranks of adulthood with a sense of vocation, an identity of our own, and an awareness of our sexuality. They will too. You can't smooth out all the sharp curves in the road. They need to master climbing their own mountains. But I'm optimistic that we can help them fare a little better than we did by not burdening our sons and daughters with the ignorance about sexuality we inherited.

THE TEEN'S WORLD: SHARED BUT APART

Teens live in the same world we do. They see the same TV shows, read the same newspapers, and go to (at least some of) the same movies. They walk or ride through the same streets; they are inhabitants of the same neighborhoods.

Mostly, though, they live in a world apart with their own music, clothes, heroes, and rituals. Specifically, they spend their days differently than do adults. Most kids spend most of their day in school. And, in school, they are segregated by grade level. They rarely interact with people of different ages and others from various socioeconomic backgrounds.

It's no news to you that teens shield themselves from the overwhelming, and often extremely critical (of them), adult society by forming a slavish devotion to their clique of other teens, who are on the same wavelength, speak the same language, and offer solace and sanctuary from school, parents, employers, and all the other older-than-18 people. Friends, in a way, form a cozy compound, much like those early pioneer wagons shielded by a tight circle from the dangers outside.

FROM SPOCK TO SHEEHY

Let's clear up one point that might be distracting. Throughout this book I refer to young people between the ages of 13 and 18 as "teens" or "teenagers," because they don't relish being called adolescents. But in the rest of this chapter, I'll mostly use the terms "adolescents" and "adolescence," because they are more descriptive of the biological and psychological transition that marks a time of life between the pediatric years delineated by Benjamin Spock and the passage years of Gail Sheehy. Keep in mind that I'm describing adolescents as a group; you need to consider the unique personality of your son or daughter.

Actually, "teenager" is a social label, and a strange one at that. While much ado is made about "teenagers" as a group, a teen as an individual (not counting their family and close relatives) is pretty much ignored or patronized by most of the adult world. Outside of some ethnic groups, no formal rite of passage takes place to mark the point in time when one crosses the threshold from child to "non-child." It's relatively simple to become a member of the teenager tribe: A person enters when they reach age 13 and exits at age 18 (somehow a 19-year-old isn't considered to be a "teenager," probably because age 18 usually marks high school graduation). For most young people, being a teenager means getting a driver's license, going on a date, drinking alcohol, earning money by getting a part-time job, decorating their own room, sitting at the grown-ups' table on holidays.

Yet it's really a gross oversimplification to lump all people between the ages of 13 and 18 under the same stereotypical label, be that teenagers or adolescents. Individual persons biologically mature on their own inner schedule, and develop their own unique personalities. Constantly remind yourself to peel away the superficial characteristics of those tagged "teenagers" and look for the individuals struggling to find themselves and their places in the world of other people. At the same time, we can recognize that young people do share a common ground of many similar feelings and body changes because they are going through the same biological-social-psychological phases of development.

DEFINING ADOLESCENCE

Just as the terms "sex" and "sexuality" are misused interchangeably, so are "adolescence" and "puberty": puberty comes from the Latin *pubere* meaning to grow over with hair, adolescence from *adolescere* meaning to grow up. Although adolescence is linked to puberty, the terms differ conceptually and chronologically.

Puberty signifies a biological process of sexual and reproductive maturation. In girls, female hormones stimulate menarche, breast development, and the fatty tissue around the hips. Endocrine activity in boys stimulates an increase in the size of the testes and penis, produces sperm, and begins the expansion of the shoulders and chest. By itself, biology will never entirely explain adolescence because, in the last analysis, adolescence is created and defined by culture. It is a complex phenomenon that varies according to an individual's life history, physical makeup, and the environment in which he or she grows up. There is little question that adolescence begins at the age of puberty, but the end of it is less certain.

There is, however, one certainty: The physical and sexual changes of adolescence are inevitable; we all went through them, and so will our sons or daughters. Hormonal changes can affect the ability to concentrate, and they can trigger new sleep patterns, huge appetites, and wild mood swings. Girls start their periods, boys have wet dreams. Voices crack. Pubic hair looks wispy. Skin breaks out. Changes in height and shape seem to happen overnight. And the need to be "normal" looms greatly. Being the first or last one to develop facial hair or breasts, or get one's period, can be devastating. Says Beth, who is 14, "All of my friends wear a bra. They call me 'little baby' because I don't have anything on top. It is really embarrassing. Do you think I should get a bra and stuff it with cotton balls?"

Waiting for the phone to ring after a first date, calling a girl for the first time, wondering whether to hold hands, and the confusion about who should pay for the movies are *daily* causes for tears, headaches, and irregular eating.

THE STAGES

The best way to understand adolescence is to put it into the context of a process, one that goes through phases and tasks. It's nearly impossible to delineate this process by age because of individual variances. It makes more sense to examine it as three stages: early, middle, and late adolescence.

In early adolescence (the "Who am I?" stage), a need for intimacy develops, relationships with same-sex peers become very important, and curiosity about sex, love, and dirty jokes becomes intense; those in early adolescence fear being different, are preoccupied with themselves, and begin to test the limits of independence. They are, in a single word, twitchy.

Middle adolescents ("Who might I be?") tend to be sensitive to maleness and femaleness, and are self-conscious about their appearance. It is usually in this stage that females begin menarche (the onset of menstruation) and males begin ejaculation and the growth spurt. Sexual identity begins to form with a strong need for peer acceptance —it sets their standards for behavior, dress, and what's in and what's out. Dating is more experimentation than involvement, with a lot of short-term "boyfriends" and "girlfriends." This is a time of dramatic shifts in self-concept. Major conflicts (I'll talk more about that later) can occur between you and your middle adolescent because these teens demand security and freedom all at the same time, alternating between "I don't want to talk about it" and "What do you think I should do?"

At last, the stage parents are more than ready for: late adolescence. Hormones are more in equilibrium, the menstrual cycle in females is usually regular, and males' body structure and voice changes have stabilized. Late adolescents' self-identity is more solid; it is the "I am me" stage.

Relationships with parents are transforming into a more adult exchange because they want to be accepted as adults. Conformity to their peer groups is less important.

The task of growing up shifts from seeking one's sexual identity to exploring it in a deeper way. Dating relationships take on an intimate, caring nature. Sexual feelings comprise both tender affection and attraction. Falling in love—for the first time—involves a truly intense concern for one's partner.

ABOUT BOYS, ABOUT GIRLS

At every stage of their progress, it is essential to talk to boys about girls' sexual development and vice versa. Too many schools still separate girls from boys for the "talk" on menstruation. I've talked to female students in high school who had no idea that males have wet dreams and to males who hadn't grasped the connection between the menstrual cycle and conception. In addition to the facts of life, we need to talk about the feelings each gender has about going through puberty. They appreciate knowing what is going on, and can be very sensitive. Says Janet, "I couldn't believe boys worry about their penis size. I thought they were all the same. My brother broke me up telling me how guys size each other up in the rest room." Tom, age 15, comments, "It must be terrible to have to think about getting up from a chair and having a big spot of blood on a skirt. I don't know why guys are so vulgar about a girl's having a period. They just show their ignorance."

GOOD TIMES, BAD TIMES

For some, adolescence is a time of Sturm und Drang; they are constantly in a state of turmoil. I'm probably committing heresy as far as developmental psychology is concerned, but I believe many young people take it in stride, mostly feeling easygoing and adjusted. Ann, age 16, says, "I love being a teenager. I know this is a special time of life—hanging out with my friends, being healthy, and not having all the responsibility of working on a job or raising kids. I'm getting okay grades and have a lot of fun in school—I go to all of the games and belong to the ski team. I'm looking forward to college, but for now being in high school is great."

For most (even Ann sometimes), it is a time of fluctuation, going from being elated and self-assured to being edgy and easily upset. In the morning they can smother you with hugs and kisses, and tell you "You're the greatest mom (or dad)"—they are walking on air, life looks rosy, school is terrific. Comes dusk, they are blue and hate school, and you—in teenage jargon—"are history." It is a time of transition. Yours and theirs. And if they have a brother or sister, it's a time of adjustment for them as well. Siblings can be under a lot of strain having to deal with the presence of a more physically mature and verbally sophisticated person in the home, one who alternately pushes for equal adult status and resorts to childish manipulations. Twelve-year-old Cheryl talks about her older sister (age 16): "She is a royal pain. She totally ignores me and then wants me to spend the night in her room so she can talk to me. She goes through my closet all of the time, but if I as much as put one foot in her room 'without her permission' she has a fit. I like her though, most of the time."

The point I want to emphasize here is this: No member of the family can escape being affected by the presence of a teenager, and each person must adjust in their own way to this startling process of watching someone changing before their eyes. Some of this adjustment entails changes in the demonstration of physical affection for the parent of the opposite sex, and rising competitive feelings for the parent of the same sex. And you'll have to deal with your adolescent's demands for more privacy and a revamping of the rules that govern family life.

Ironically, for some parents, their child's adolescence couldn't be more poorly timed. A majority of parents of teens are over 40, and face the physical and emotional challenges of midlife just as their children are going through their teenage crisis. Again, this isn't negative for everyone. For many parents, having a member of the family going through the teenage years smoothes over any "midlife crisis" by giving them a new lease on life.

RAGING HORMONES

What makes adolescents so edgy? All in all, adolescents' energy, chafing for independence, and mood fluctuations derive from their emerging sexual maturation.

When the glands related to the reproductive system start to manufacture and secrete into the bloodstream male or female hormones, they start a chain reaction that permeates all aspects of a teen's life, sometimes subtly and other times obviously. What is important to grasp about this surge of hormones is how it awakens the sex drive. I'm not talking about sexual desire. That is only one part of the sex drive, and I'll discuss it in the chapter on sex (Chapter 5). What I mean by "sex drive" is the basic sexual reproductive system that passes on life from one generation to the next. It is this reproductive instinct that ultimately results in the sperm of the male uniting with the ova of the female, or as it is referred to in folklore, "nature."

How much the "biological imperative" motivates people to assert themselves sexually, like so much of all aspects of human nature, isn't well understood; there are many theories but little agreement. A full discussion of the complexity of the sex drive—the genetic coding to reproduce ourselves as a species—is beyond the scope here. All I can tell you is that when you are in a roomful of adolescents the itchiness of sexual hormones pervades the atmosphere.

The sex drive impulses aren't a problem per se; they are an integral aspect of human existence. And, of course, the sex drive doesn't function independently of other human drives: to win approval and love, to achieve, to gain power and prestige, to satisfy curiosity. In a given situation, one or more of these strong impulses can temper, or even repress, the sex drive.

Adolescent sex drives become a problem—to them and to us—because as a society we either downplay them or aren't equipped to channel them. For example, there is the influence of society's lingering Victorian notions that "innocent" children should somehow not have such animalistic urges. And, living in a very technological world, we have, for the most part, become very detached from acknowledging our biological instincts.

If young people could make the transition from childhood to adulthood in one leap—could marry and become economically independent—at the time of their lives when they feel intense sex drives, adolescents would be a lot easier to deal with. But our society is not as simple as many cultures of the world where young people marry and have children at age 15 or so. Contrast our isolated nuclear families to those societies where the whole family, three generations together, combine resources and live interdependently. Our world demands academic preparation as a baseline to enter the vocational arena. We expect marriage and childbearing to be postponed until the family unit can be mostly self-sufficient. The period of adolescence has been extended a great deal beyond the development of the ability to reproduce (the most common cross-over from child to adult in other cultures) because we expect a person to assume the responsibilities and to make the kinds of decisions necessary for independent adult living before they are "on their own."

What we have, then, is that adolescent sex drives are not very straightforwardly dealt with. Their feelings are real enough all right, but because we, as a society, are not equipped to let adolescents act upon them, they find another way to express them: vague, undefined urges to go somewhere, do something—something exciting, something risky.

STRAINING AT THE LEASH

What we are really up against is this: Better nutrition, health care, and disease prevention have combined to lower the average age of menarche to less than 12 years of age in females. And a vast majority of males could father a child at age 14. Thus, your young adolescent becomes a biological "adult" while still a social neophyte and an economic infant. And what we are stuck with is this: adolescents straining at the leash. This push-pull tug-of-war between biology and culture is one of the most potent but least recognized reasons for parent and teen conflict—especially when they are of the same sex.

Sons and fathers can lock horns like two bull moose trying to establish supremacy. Take, for instance, the complaint of Bill, age 16, about his father's tight rein of authority: "My dad doesn't even try to understand how I need the car just to cruise around in. I feel cooped up, like a prisoner, when I have to stick around the house all night. But when I ask to use the car, he gets all intense. 'Why do you have to go out? Where are you going? Stay home and study.' He loves to play the boss of the house. But I'm getting so tired of being under his thumb like a baby. I can't wait until I have my own wheels and don't have to kowtow to Mr. Big." I'm sure Bill's dad isn't thrilled about constantly being confronted and challenged. Nothing is more difficult than to remember how much we, as teens, hated to toe the line, explain our need to get out, to see and be seen.

Check out the "main drag" in your town (or the "in" place in your city) and you'll observe teens in a peacock parade: slow-cruising cars, or walking on the sidewalk, strutting, going up and down, around and around—seeking excitement, stalking the night long after we yearn to click off the TV and get a good night's sleep.

The discordant note of "independence" before "maturity" may find your teen acting sour, or downright ugly, toward you for no apparent rational reason. Somehow, daughters seem more prone to act that way toward mothers than any other combination of parent-child relationship. Sexual competition? I don't know. I do know the relationship between a young teenage daughter and her mother is, from time to time, very tense. A mother can feel she needs to tiptoe on eggshells around her daughter. For example, the following scene: Daughter is wearing a path between the mirror and her closet, becoming more and more frantic because she can't make up her mind about what to wear on a date. She asks her mom for her opinion about the "pink sweater with the white skirt." Unsuspecting, Mom says, "That always looks great on you." Daughter angrily replies, "It looks really stupid. You don't understand anything." Sometimes we are damned if we are helpful and damned if we aren't.

When you become really annoyed at your teen's petulance, try to temper your immediate response. Their edginess may not be personal at all. When the sex hormones begin to appear they play a direct role in an adolescent's tendency to have emotional flip-flops—to seem, alternately, so lethargic or so wired or ready for combat. Chalk it up to adolescent spring fever, part of the great scheme of Mother (Father?) Nature.

I'm not implying that "raging hormones" be used as an excuse to get teens off the hook every time they are rude, nasty, or neglectful. Your son or daughter should be expected to play fair, treat people decently, and carry their own weight. I'm suggesting that, before you become angry, or hurt, you put their actions into perspective, to preserve your own sanity. Maybe what is going on makes sense, at least in a way. You are playing the historical, generational king-of-the-mountain game: On their move they resent arbitrary authority; on your move you resent impertinence and rebellion. Your son or daughter may simply be trying to push you to the edge to see how far they can go: the challenge of the sexually primed warriors to the constraints imposed by the tribal clders.

TWO STEPS FORWARD, ONE STEP BACK

It is kind of a setup. Feeling unsure of themselves, they feel unsure about us, which means that sometimes they reject the very advice they seem so needy for. But the desire for independence isn't constant. There is an occasional step backward. All of this adds up to tension between you and your almost-adult/almost-child adolescent. Our expectations are virtually impossible to synchronize. When they want to be treated as an adult, we want to hang on to their fading childhood. When we wish they would act "grown-up," they cling to childhood like a security blanket. Trying to communicate with a teen can be a wary two-step. Forward to closeness, retreat to confrontation. Treat them like a child, they feel patronized; treat them like an adult, they feel anxious.

A good way to handle this forward/backward motion is to see it for what it is: part of the long haul to adulthood. Intense though these times are, they soon will pass unless you get all snarled up in them. Tolerance, yours for them, them for you, can smooth over many a rough moment. My kids and I developed a way of laying out the ground rules for family disagreements that helped (most of the time) to keep us focused on trying to settle our differences. Because I don't respond very well to pouty behavior, I ask them to try to be a little more upbeat in presenting their case, "to lighten up." They, in turn, when I get, as they call it, "bent out of shape," issue the same request. I know how silly this exchange sounds, but somehow it reduces the tension and we can talk things over without being distracted and infuriated with each other's attitude.

Keep in mind that adolescents are confronted with enormous psychosexual changes over a relatively short period of time, given the length of our life's calendar. Lamented one adolescent male, "I never look the same two days in a row." And because they aren't sure that there is life after high school, it seems forever. Hence, there is a major division between teen and adult: We have gained control over many (not all) of our emotional reactions to life's disappointments, and have enough experience to know that tomorrow is another day. Teenagers don't have this perspective. Their reactions to everyday achievements or disappointments are usually very melodramatic and self-centered. Even when their problems or reactions seem trivial or off the wall, be patient and empathetic.

LIVING THROUGH YOUR ADOLESCENT'S ADOLESCENCE

Keep reminding yourself that the major task of adolescence is to form an individual's sense of identity while separating from their parents. It can be exasperating because they are often highly critical of us—putting down our suggestions, pointing out our shortcomings. Take comfort in knowing that these rebels *have* a cause: the task of growing up. Before you know it they'll be young adults and you'll have a lot of "war stories" to share and laugh over together.

Essential to a good relationship between you and your teen is a sense of emotional rapport and mutual respect for each other. If you can, no matter what, operate with these as the basics of your communication, you can't go wrong.

SELF-ESTEEM

Help your teen develop a positive sense of sexuality by bolstering their self-esteem. Their quest for self-identity is too often bogged down by a low opinion of themselves. But don't give them false praise. Teens can see through, and resent, our efforts (no matter how well meaning) to pat them on the back with more enthusiasm than the situation calls for. They need to know they are okay, that you appreciate them and their efforts, but go easy. It's a natural parental reflex to heap praise upon our child to show our love, but reserve it for situations that really merit it. Teens say they don't want to be complemented for ordinary accomplishments ("Oh, you are using your knife so well!"), or for their looks ("You have the cutest dimples!").

They scorn appreciation not genuinely earned and thrive on honest and realistic applause. Says Alice, age 16, "I'm not a great dancer, just so-so. I've been taking lessons since I was 6. I enjoy it and love being in the dance shows, but I'm not exactly, you know, a natural talent. Everytime my dance studio puts on a program, I could dig a hole and bury myself to get away from my mother. For days and days she tells everyone we know what a terrific dancer I am, and is constantly telling me, 'You are the *best* dancer.' I've tried to explain that I'll never be on Broadway or Carnegie Hall and I can live with that. But she runs her mouth about how I could go to the top of the heap without hearing me."

I'm not saying don't lavish praise, but be clear about what you are praising. For example, I think Alice might be more receptive to her mother's enthusiasm for her dancing if she said: "I love to see you dance; it gives me great pleasure and I'm happy you are doing something you really enjoy." This way Alice can enjoy dancing and her mother's applause because it fits the situation.

Self-esteem develops from the capacity for liking yourself and accepting yourself—a general all-round positive energy about who you are. Few people are able to acquire much self-esteem in the early and middle years of adolescence, but, with a good foundation, by late adolescence you'll see your son or daughter bloom.

THE POT OF GOLD

I've said a lot about the challenge and the confusion inherent in raising a teen, because it is a help to know what to expect, or to know you're not alone in wondering how to handle the situation. I really think there are more sizable rewards than problems. Let's not lose sight of how much fun, most of the time, it is.

The parent of a teen is usually the object almost of pity, deluged with dire warnings. Typical is: "You just wait. When they are little, your problems are little, but your problems get bigger as they get bigger." Have you noticed how no one seems to *envy* you as the parent of a teen? My advice is to not let other people's glum predictions or expectations color your experience.

The root of disgruntlement may be the assumption, on the part of some people, that all teens are as objectionable as they are usually portrayed in the media—the teenager as bad seed, crazed out-of-control maniac, or whiny wimp-ola who constantly screws up. Whatever the reasons for so much bad press about raising a teen, most parents, myself included, don't feel put-out or put-upon at all. Let me go on record and say that few teenagers are the troublemakers or the harbingers of doom and gloom the media so stereotypically portray them to be.

I enjoyed each of my kids' teen years. I liked them and their friends; they added a real plus to my life and still do. Glo, owner of a bookstore, mother of three, is one of the many parents I interviewed who talked about how much they enjoyed their children's teenage years—for Glo, from her daughters a few years ago to her son who is now 15. She put it this way: "I love my teenagers. Too much is said about how dreadful this period is and how disruptive and almost impossible teens are to deal with. It's just too negative. Maybe for some families, but most everyone I know raising a teen seems to be doing it with relative ease. For myself, I enjoy each of my kids immensely. They are so interesting, I can't imagine life without them." Another parent, Kay, who has two teenage sons, told me, "They are a bundle of energy. They both make me wonder at the world all over again. I love to sit around and talk to my kids and their friends. They are a breath of fresh air."

A bonus from having a teen is that they are a real antidote to feeling gloomy. Their enthusiasm adds a lot of spark to our existence. Having an adolescent in the house means having the walls vibrate with music and chatter, underscored by the bustle of activities from an ever-changing scene of young people.

Their interest in things—computers, dance, orchestra, sports, photography, art, vegetarianism—can spark for us a renewed interest, or introduce us to something new. They are your in-house anchorperson, keeping you up on the news and trends in popular music, literature, and fashion. Because they are shrewd analysts of character and social events they give us a different perspective from what we get from our friends.

And they can be irresistibly funny. With their uninhibited sense of humor, they love to give us the straight scoop about the comings and goings of family, neighborhood, and the world as they see it. They make us chuckle at our own shortcomings, or at least make us take another look. I remember the time when my son Don added his two cents' worth to a dinner table conversation about "phoniness" and my distaste for "phony" people. With gestures and tone he carefully mimicked the remarkable change in my demeanor that had taken place earlier that day when a phone call from one of my friends interrupted a "talk" I was giving him about his lack of responsibility about getting the garbage (make that "the damn garbage") out to the curb for pickup: "Ohhh, hellooo, how *are* you? No, I'm not busy." Me? A phony?

Or my son John, in a stage whisper meant to reach the balcony, telling a new friend when they came in the front door, "Watch out for my mom's questions, she is really grilling you for a book—after we split she writes down everything you say." And I thought I was too smart to get caught.

Think of it this way: No more babysitters, they are not dependent upon you for dressing and feeding, and they can carry on a conversation to boot. Enjoy them—time is fleeting. They are only teens for six years or so, and they are pretty special.

A SUMMARY OF THE FACTS

• Hormones control the onset and course of puberty, but it's not fully understood what causes the hypothalamus gland to initiate that chain of events. At some point shortly before puberty, the hypothalamus triggers increased secretions of gonadotropin (follicle-stimulating hormone, FSH, and luteinizing hormone, LH) from the pituitary gland, which in turns causes increased production of sex hormones. Pubertal changes are the result of the increased output of these sex hormones by the gonads and adrenal cortex.

• Most boys develop later than most girls. The adolescent growth spurt for boys usually begins at about age 12. The peak rate in height growth is reached at about age 14. (Remember "about" and "usually.")

• In girls, the growth spurt starts about two years earlier, at about 8 to 10 years, reaching a peak rate at around 12 years. It is interesting to note that, although children have been growing taller and heavier and maturing earlier over the years, this two-year difference between the sexes in the timing of the growth spurt has not changed.

• In boys, the growth spurt is accompanied by rapid development of the reproductive organs: enlargement of the testes and reddening and wrinkling of the scrotum. Pubic hair may begin to appear now, but usually it comes in somewhat later.

• The first ejaculation of seminal fluid generally occurs about a year after the start of the penile growth spurt. Wet dreams (nocturnal emissions) usually begin at about age 14.

• Growth in stature for most males is completed by age 18 to 19, but some continue at a slower rate to gain height throughout the early 20s.

• As a rule, the first sign of puberty for girls, at about age 10 or 11, is the appearance of the breast bud. The nipples become enlarged, followed by growth around the nipples. Girls need to know that breast size depends upon heredity and weight, that breasts come in all sizes and shapes, and that they are never evenly matched. Some nipples are inverted, and the breast can be lumpy. (Any change in breast tissue, or if a lump stays in place for several weeks, needs to be checked out by a clinician.) This is a very important subject to talk about because, whether we like it or not, a woman's breasts are a great sexual symbol in our society. So, girls (and, later, women) spend a lot of time wishing their breasts were bigger, smaller, or shaped differently. Try to help your daughter (and your son) understand that breast size has nothing to do with sexual capacity, nor does it affect a woman's ability to breast-feed. While you're on the topic it won't hurt to point out that breasts are not a sign of intelligence or a lack of brain power.

• The average age for menarche (beginning of the menstrual cycle) is about 12 years, which means some girls will start menstruating around age 10 and others at 15. Usually three-quarters of the way between the beginning and the end of a girl's growth spurt and sexual development she'll begin menstruation. And this event, the first sight of menstrual blood, is very significant. Every woman can remember her first period. Make it a happy moment, not one of fear, embarrassment, or disgust. It needs to be a celebrated sign of approaching womanhood. I recommend that girls by age 8 know all about menstruation and have a kit of junior-size tampons and minipads. This way there won't be any surprises. By the way, thick sanitary napkins are not used much anymore. They're too bulky and they get in the way for girls who are a lot more active in sports than in the olden days. Don't hesitate to instruct your daughter in how to use tampons correctly, she'll manage fine. And who cares about her having an intact hymen?

NOTE: If for any reason you feel concerned that something is not going right in your son's or daughter's development, it is a good idea to take them to a clinician for a checkup.

CHAPTER FOUR

WHAT IS THIS THING CALLED LOVE?

REMEMBER PULLING OUT DAISY PETALS—loves me, loves me not—crossing out letters in each other's names, seeking fortune tellers, reading cards or tea leaves, and endlessly grilling all of your friends trying to find out if "he" (or "she") *really* loved you? I'll bet your daughter or son is doing one or more of the above for the very same reason. Teenage love feelings are still, and no doubt will always be, mixed up and intense, seesawing between a marvelous sunshiny burst of happiness and a stormy cloud of despair.

Love is so personal, yet so universal—what can we say? We feel a tremendous responsibility to frame the words eloquently. We don't want to give our teen the impression that love is elusive or beyond explanation, nor do we want to attribute it to the whimsical simplicity of Cupid aiming his arrow at an unsuspecting lover. Love has a tremendous impact on our lives, and the need to love and be loved is enormous. We know it is an essential facet of human existence. But it is so complex, and has so many shades of meanings, that our first instinct (yes, me too) is to leap to the bookshelf to find the perfect quote that will say exactly what we want to say, only better. And what do we discover? Endless and contradictory observations on the nature of "love" have been made by poets, philosophers, behaviorists, and simpler folk. Despite the outpouring of ink, words, tears, and even venom on the subject, a precise definition of love, one that all of us can nod our heads in agreement with, doesn't exist. Still, I'm sure you have a classic or two that you cherish because they express your thoughts nearly perfectly.

It is useful to lean on the wisdom of the sages; I can't resist sprinkling some of the quotes I think are worth repeating here in this chapter. But don't overdo it. Pithy phrases and stirring literary creations about LOVE tend to put teenagers to sleep. They find most of it too abstract, too wordy.

Teens don't want to hear about the philosophy of love; they want some practical advice about how to know if you are "really" in love, and an explanation of how to cope with being "head over heels." They want to know if loving someone means you want to have sex with them, and they want to know why sometimes you love someone but that person doesn't feel exactly the same about you.

Articulating the special qualities and differences between "liking," "infatuation," "loving," and "real love" to a teen is taxing, at best. Teens tell me parents get a serious look on their faces, babble on and on, or cut the conversation short muttering something like, "Someday . . . you'll know." Apparently, we rarely get to the point, nor do we explain anything close to what our son or daughter is dying to find out. Usually, I find that parents neglect to make any relevant connection between "love" and "lust" when they discuss the topic of love with their teen. This could be a holdover from our conditioning that love is pure and sex isn't, or an attempt to shield young people from the earthier aspects of romance. Maybe in many instances it's simple reluctance because we're on shaky ground.

Nevertheless, give it a try, because, for all of the conflicting opinion about what is or isn't love, and in spite of the lack of research data, we all know intuitively that "it" exists. While few of us can lay claim to being totally rational about the state, or art, of love, loving, and being loved, at least we've had more experience than our young. That *has* to count for something. However, know before you begin that, no matter how much you talk to them about the wonders and risks of "falling in love" or "being in love," in the final analysis, to understand it, they will have to experience it for themselves. All you can hope to do is to lend them some insight.

It's a good idea to tell them, right at the start, that no one has all the answers. People are so complex, and the forces that attract them to each other are so complicated, that it is never easy to unmask one's own feelings. However, we can at least provide some guidance about distinguishing between the emotions and relationships involved in infatuation (crushes), romantic attraction ("chemistry"), and the loving attachment (companionate love) that grows between two people over time. This will go a long way in enabling them to become more aware of what they need and expect from "love," and to consider how their desires might fit or collide with those of another person.

LOVE WORDS

Let's begin with the word *love* itself. Of all the words in the English language, it is perhaps the most open to interpretation. When it's used in the phrase "I love you," it can mean any number of things and be interpreted in any number of ways. "I love you" may mean to one person "I need you" when what they meant was "I want you to need me."

To another person it may mean "I desire you sexually"; to still another it may mean "I want to belong to you" or "I like you a whole lot." Some people use the word to describe something else. They say they are "in love" instead of saying "I'm attracted to you," "My heart's in my throat," "I'm horny," or "I'm very intrigued." Others invest the word *love* with such weighty meaning that they hesitate to use it at all, because, to their way of thinking, the word when spoken, as in "I love you," is an irreversible commitment, a verbal contract binding one person to another forever.

When a person is greatly threatened by the intense emotions and responsibility they associate with the word *love*, they avoid it at all costs, or resort to substituting words such as "care for," "respect," or "adore," which to them do not convey the same menace as the "L" word. Then, other people toss the word *love* around casually. They say "I love you" to another person before they know how to spell the person's last name.

Steer your teen clear of making assumptions about love. Encourage them, when using love words, to do two things: clarify for themselves what they mean when they say love, or "I love you," and never take for granted that they are on the same wavelength as someone else.

T.G.A.L.S.

However, before you can focus your teen's attention on how to recognize love in its different forms and intensities, you'll have to ring down the curtain on the longest-running myth about love ever invented. This is the captivating saga of True Love: two perfectly matched people fated to meet and love each other—forever and ever. You may have forgotten, or blocked it, so to refresh your memory:

THE GREAT AMERICAN LOVE STORY
(with a tip of the hat to Evelyn M. Duvall)

SCENE ONE: She is sweet, good-looking, nice. She does okay in school, gets along fine with her family, and has a lot of friends. She is busy doing things and going places. But she is vaguely discontented, longing for The Real Thing. Sometimes she meets a guy she likes a lot, but nothing comes of it because she is waiting for HIM. Someday, some way, they'll find each other.

SCENE TWO: He appears. He knows that SHE is for HIM. He is tall, handsome, but slightly shy. Her heart pounds rapidly. She can't take her eyes off HIM. Everyone around them knows that THEY are meant for each other. After a few anxious moments trying to meet each other, they talk for hours.

SCENE THREE: They fall in LOVE, suddenly, without reservations. Before, life had little real meaning. She was an unclaimed treasure. Now, in this scant moment, her life has changed. She is transformed into a woman, a woman loved by a wonderful guy. Before he found her he was not unhappy, but now he knows what has been lacking in his life—a woman who truly loves him. One who will stick by his side through hell and high water, bring out his best qualities, and help him make something of himself.

SCENE FOUR: They must be together every moment. Not a minute goes by that they don't think of each other . . . long for each other. Each kiss, each embrace is thrilling, special. They know that there is, in all of the world, only one man for one woman. They tell each other how lucky they are to have found each other.

THE FINAL SCENE: They live happily ever after. They are lifetime sweethearts, with never a cross word or a dull moment, bound together by the never-ending bliss of belonging to each other.

As laughable, if not downright pitiful, as this oft-told tale seems to you, don't dismiss it as too silly to be taken seriously by the current crop of teenagers. Even as they put it down as totally outdated and ridiculous, they can't help being influenced by it, at least to some degree. The romantic script of True Love—that lovers will somehow know when they truly find the right person, and that genuine love is eternal—is a revered tradition in our cultural folklore. It is what every young boy and girl hear in songs, movies, and advertisements, and read in books and magazines. Most teens, who are optimists anyway, want to believe it *can* happen to them, despite all evidence to the contrary. And, come to think of it, I know some grown-ups who still have their hopes up.

Now that you have debunked the notion that True Love exists, you can move on to what is realistic. An exhaustive list of hard data on the subject isn't available, but from the common ground of people's experiences and observations love can be described in terms of cycles or phases. This doesn't mean that love can be neatly categorized, or that each of us experiences love in a predictable, sequential process. Rather, it gives us a way to organize our thinking. Although the lines between these phases are difficult to draw, and can overlap, isolating each phase for purposes of discussion is far better than having to resort to telling your teen: "Love is, well, a mystery."

THE WHIRLWIND

Infatuation is that hit-me-like-a-ton-of-bricks feeling—being wildly fascinated by another person whom you don't really know for the person they are. Because it is an attraction that is based on an abstraction of the person and the relationship—a fantasy—it rarely survives once reality intrudes. Being infatuated is a quirky kind of emotion. It comes on strong and goes just as quickly. This feeling has been called anything from "puppy" love, or "raging hormones," to "counterfeit" love. It is a powerful emotion, and very seductive. Knowing the difference between being infatuated and falling in love is virtually impossible while it's happening—the distinction is usually made in retrospect.

There are a few clues you can share with your teen to help them key in a little earlier. Psychologist Dorothy Tennov coined a word, "limerence," to describe when this head-over-heels zinging feeling becomes an affliction as well as a joy. Limerence is marked by preoccupation with the love object to the detriment of other aspects of your life. The limerent lover's mood depends upon the actions and desires of the loved one; you hang on their every word, hoping for approval and fearing rejection. Another hint is that, once you begin to see each other frequently, the excitement wears thin. You argue about every little thing. One person almost always is more "infatuated" than the other, and jealousy causes a lot of pain. As the bubble is bursting, you see faults in the other person you didn't see before. Now what was charming about them seems to ring a false note, or becomes annoying. Recalling how this happened to her, Jan, age 17, says, "He turned out to be more ordinary than I thought. More shallow, no real depth. I still thought he was cute, but it wasn't enough."

FALLING, FALLING IN LOVE

Romantic attraction is the unexplicable magnetism that draws one person to another. Something about another person, the way he or she walks, or talks, the curl of their hair—any one of a million little things trips off an intense attraction to them. Your eyes and thoughts gravitate toward them. You want to be with them, talk to them. You can't think of anything else. Most of all you want that person to want you, to be "in love" with you. Unlike infatuation, although initially it feels much the same, romantic attraction isn't based on a fantasy. The person is seen for who they are (albeit the lenses are very rosy) and you both feel the same way about each other.

This intoxication, the giddy, breathless onrush of romantic desires fermenting in an atmosphere of sexually charged excitement, is what people call "falling in love."

Romantic attraction is, by any measure, one effervescent wonderful feeling. However mystical its essence, some researchers in the newly emerging science of the chemistry of emotions believe it is a physiochemical experience too. Dr. Michael Liebowitz, author of *The Chemistry of Love*, says the feeling of "electrical" attraction is reflected in actual brain activity. He theorizes that when people experience what is commonly recognized as "falling in love" a chemical chain reaction is triggered by the appearance of a person who fits an unconscious image of a desirable mate, and this makes your pulse race and your heart leap. This particular brain chemical is called phenylethylamine and it's been identified as the neurochemical responsible for the feelings of elation, exhilaration, and euphoria that we experience when falling in love. But this doesn't mean that science can reduce the wonders of love to some pharmaceutical formula.

Untangling the link between sexual chemistry and our feelings of romantic love needn't be construed to mean that phenylethylamine is love itself, only that it seems responsible for the conscious experience of at least some of the symptoms of romance. No one is more in awe of the power and puzzling veils of love than I. Yet I find that teens are fascinated and receptive to learning about how romantic responses might very well be activated and recharged through biochemical processes. You can be skeptical or not, but explore it with your son or daughter. It goes a long way in explaining why romantic attraction gives lovers that transcendent feeling, a feeling beyond time, space, and your own body. And it puts in perspective the fact that affairs of the heart are not so simple, that they are a combination of intellect, hormones, and maybe even luck.

Still, for all of the rich lore of personal anecdotes, and the discovery of the "molecule of love," falling in love seems to be an emotional experience that feels unique to each person and strains rational discussion. Never try to convince your teen, if they are in the midst of romantic attraction, that this all-engrossing "in love" feeling for another person isn't The Real Thing. It is to them. They will assume (a) you simply have forgotten what love is all about or (b) you have never felt that way. Try to key in on the fact that being romantically enthralled is only one of the steps couples go through in a relationship and that, while it is terrific, it isn't the final inning. It's love all right, but love has other moments, other stages.

CUDDLY, COMFORTING LOVERS

Point out that it is difficult to maintain the intensity of romantic energy on a consistent basis over time. The initial romance either fades eventually or moves on to another level where you are genuinely happy in a warm blissful way and feel that initial excitement only once in a while. Instead of toasting with champagne on the Staten Island Ferry, or dreaming about being alone on a tropical island, you are content to curl up together watching "Dallas" or an old movie.

Feeling pleased with yourself at having unscrambled the

love maze? It's a little too soon to rest on your laurels. Teens won't let you off the hook that easily. They find the possibility of romantic love tapering off, or reappearing in the coziness of "His and Her" coffee cups, difficult to imagine. It "won't" or "can't" happen to them. They usually attribute a lapse in romantic attraction to a syndrome of old age, or the plight of other couples "less in love." You may not be able to bridge the span of their disbelief, but you can answer their most common questions: "Why does this happen?" "Does it have to go that way?" Alas, the answer is yes, even to the most ardent of lovers. Assure them that doesn't mean romantic attraction goes away completely. For many couples, as they continue their relationship, the romance mostly goes into low gear, occasionally returning to a high level of intensity.

As for why, there isn't any one reason. Maybe in the natural progression of being around another person familiarity takes the edge off the thrill of the unknown. It could be that it is too distracting, and we need to switch gears to a calmer, more settled-in relationship to maintain the survival of the species, or simply move on to other aspects of our life. Dr. Liebowitz thinks neurochemistry plays a role in the more relaxed feelings felt by a couple when they have been lovers for a while. He describes the next stage—that day-in, day-out intimacy of loving commitment—as "attachment," which is often associated with a lessening of anxiety, because it involves another set of chemical reactions in the body. Rather than the amphetamine-like substances, the brain produces a group of soothing chemicals that are secreted when a person is in a comfortable, secure situation. "I don't think it is . . . an accident," Liebowitz explains, "that great romances of literature such as Romeo and Juliet, or Cathy and Heathcliff, occur between people who, for one reason or another, don't have a chance to stay together. Their brain pleasure center (where phenylethylamine is produced) has not had time to get used to, and is therefore less excited by, having the other person around."

INTIMACY AND LOVE

Without waxing too lyrical, discuss with your teen how we learn to love through the experience of loving. We love another person for different reasons, and the reasons vary over time. Mostly, loving another and being loved by them in return means we meet each other's needs or we satisfy one another's expectations of belongingness. When love is based on positive feelings about ourselves and the other person it is a loyal friendly feeling, called companionate love.

Simply, while you initially "fall" in love with another person, in a real sense you "grow" into love, both as individuals and as a couple. This kind of love isn't inferior to romantic love, nor is it dull and predictable. Rather, a companionate relationship is made of sturdier stuff than romantic attraction because it is based on sharing, trust, and being friends more than on the intensity of passion. The sexual feelings remain, but more like a flame that sometimes blazes than like an always-present raging fire.

Dr. Harold Bessell, a well-known consultant on emotional and mental health, gives us a useful description of the kind of love of which we all dream. He says it is a combination of romantic love (the electric sexual spark that sets a friendship on fire) and emotional maturity (the ability to be aware of one's own emotions and motivations, the capability to behave in constructive ways to attain your desires, and the integrity to relate to the other person honestly, affectionately, and considerately). He makes sense to me. But I would put a little more weight on the contribution of the "electric sexual spark" than he does.

To my thinking, passion is an essential ingredient. It

doesn't have to be ever-present, but sexual compatibility is the taproot of a long-lasting loving relationship. The sensuousness of romantic attraction along with the comfort of companionate love is what I would call "real" love. Simply put, love is a friendship, sparked by sexual chemistry, that grows over time.

MORE ON THE LOVE CONDITION

One of the hardest things for teens, especially young teens, to comprehend is that "real" love is mutual. It isn't love unless the devotion is shared equally by two partners. If it's one-sided, it's infatuation. Tell them that romantic attraction can't be created or forced, because it is a deep biopsychological force. It's either there or it's not.

Noted sex educator Sol Gordon provides another way to help teens sort out infatuation from something more. He says, "if you are in love, you are," but that there are two kinds: "Mature love is when caring about the other person is just a little more important than having the other person care for you. This kind of relationship makes both partners feel better. Mature love is playful, passionate, sensitive, and proud. Both partners have a lot of energy. Immature love is when it is much more important to have the other person care for you than it is for you to care for the other person. This kind of relationship often feels like a burden. It is exhausting because it involves more taking than giving. There is a lot of jealousy, bickering, and meanness, and many apologies."

LOVE HAS MANY FACES

Another point that is difficult for young people to grasp is that love doesn't come just once in a lifetime. Urge them to expect to be in love many times. Without sounding cynical, let them know that, until you've reached a certain point of knowing who you are, what you want for yourself, and what you are willing to give in a relationship, the love felt is for now, but not likely forever. For romantic attraction to endure and emerge into companionate love takes hard work, practice, and a willingness to compromise and communicate under ever-changing circumstances. Most romantic attraction relationships are not cut out for that. But that doesn't make the relationship not worthwhile. It is.

Debunk the notion that when you love someone something must be done about it. It must lead to something else. It's not so surprising that teens are not content with love existing in the status quo. They hear the same theme we did in the song "Love and Marriage." Many teens feel that unless future plans are made—anything from being promised to being engaged to something more formal—their partner isn't displaying all of the signs of "being serious." While longing for commitment when you are wrapped up in feelings of romantic attraction is a natural response, for teens "commitment" needs to be redefined. Commitment can be for now, an agreement between two people. That doesn't make a love relationship between teens a sorry substitute for that experienced by adults when they decide to live together or get married. What teens feel is real to them. Encourage them to enjoy it. As one parent put it, "I told my son that love is one of the best feelings in the world. He's lucky to find someone he cares for so much, and someone who feels the same about him. If it's for only today—terrific. If it lasts for several tomorrows—fine, fine. Enjoy it for however long it lasts." My message to my kids, and the teens I talk with, is very much the same as that parent's, with a footnote: It's wonderful to lose your heart, just don't lose your head.

It may not sink in, given how love-smitten a teen can be, but toss another thought into their mental computer anyway: As marvelous as love is, it's not a road map to eternal happiness. It's great. But it's not the end all or be all.

WHEN YOUR TEEN FALLS IN LOVE

The best time to bring up the wonders and the ups and downs of love is when your teen isn't madly in love. They are more apt to pay attention. But if that is already happening to them, forge on anyway. Don't put the focus on whom they "love" and their specific relationship unless they want to talk about it. Teens can become very defensive very quickly. Sometimes they react that way as a reflex, but sometimes parents put them in that position. Why? Because it's hard to be objective about the person who has great influence over our son or daughter. No matter how delighted a parent is that their son or daughter is experiencing the feelings of loving and being loved, we watch a little fearfully as our vulnerable offspring give their heart to a stranger.

What makes many parents a bit anxious about the role of the "lover" in their son's or daughter's life is the worry about how the relationship will affect their future. We envision a premature walk up the aisle at best, and at worst a high school dropout. Teens can become so caught up with being in love that nothing else seems to matter. It is hard to sit on the sidelines and watch their interest in hanging out with friends, or in sports or studying, dwindle away. You want them to have the experience of being involved in a loving relationship, but not to the extent of making the other person the centerpiece in their life. It's not a frivolous worry. Teens seem to suspend their good sense when in the throes of love. For example, let me tell you what happened when one of my sons fell madly in love while in high school. He became reluctant to spend any time with anyone but the girl he was going with, and generally took less interest in school activities and most of the comings and goings of family life. I was not happy seeing him become so absorbed, but kept my fingers crossed it would eventually taper off. It did, but not before he racked up a huge phone bill when he went away for a month on a sports program. Long after the love affair ended he was still paying that bill (read "*damn* bill"). And every payment rekindled the tension between us over the fact that he had accrued it in the first place. I was caught between being sympathetic to his heartbroken feelings and the urge to wring his neck, not to mention my distress at the price he paid in grades and the camaraderie of high school pals. (He recovered okay, and found another love in college.)

For most of us, there is another problem. Sometimes it isn't so easy to step gracefully aside as the apple of your child's eye: to relinquish the role of someone they looked up to, admired, wanted to spend time with, especially when they indeed appear to be "blinded by love." Phil, the father of a 16-year-old daughter, put it this way: "When my daughter went out on dates with a group of kids, I was delighted. I liked all of the boys that were part of the crowd. But now it's one-on-one. And the guy is a jerk. When my daughter walks out the door I feel I'm risking 16 years of raising her for that idiot. I can't believe my own feelings!"

It is much easier to accept the fact that our son or daughter is "in love" when the person they are wild about is someone we like. Admittedly, when they bring home a clean-cut, well-mannered, nice-looking person with a sense of humor and ambitious plans for a career, we feel we can relax. But when the person has a personality that grates on us or has a set of characteristics we deem questionable, it becomes hard to dust off the welcome mat.

MR./MS. WRONG

If you really dislike the person your teen is enamored with, try to keep it in perspective. Don't speak too soon. It may be nothing more than a passing fancy. If not, engrave the following rule into your mind: Never harshly criticize the person they are in love with. As teens admonish me: "Tell parents not to bad-mouth him/her." Some teens say that, no matter how terrific the person is that they are in love with, their parents don't seem to totally approve. Your disapproval can make them decide to be secretive about what they really feel for that person. Or they might tag you as a parent who "doesn't really understand." Whatever, the result is the same. It only widens the gap between you and your son or daughter. They can get defensive, and further communication on the topic becomes tense, if not impossible.

It is better to discuss the other person's good points and then talk about what it is about them that concerns you. Keep cool. Don't issue ultimatums; they are a futile gesture. Forbidding your teen to continue the relationship can lead to sneaking around. It's not that teens want to be underhanded, but they may resort to that kind of behavior when they think a parent is unfair, closed-minded, or wrong. Says June, age 16: "My parents are always on my back about Kevin [age 19]. My mom thinks he is stupid and my dad can't say a civil word to him. They say he is irresponsible and too old for me. They just don't know him the way I do. He's shy and quits jobs because he is going to school part-time and is always looking for something that pays a little more or will give him more time off when he has tests and stuff. But now things have gotten really bad. My mom says I have to break up with him and date some guys my own age. I can't do that. I really love Kevin. I tell them I'm going to study or visit friends so I can be with him. My friends know all about it and say they'll cover for me if they have to."

And reports Amy, age 17: "My parents didn't like the guy I was going with last summer—all they did was put him down. So I pretended I wasn't interested in him anymore. I just didn't talk about him around the house. When I went out we usually were with our friends and when my parents asked me who was going, I would say this one and that one, but I left out the guy's name. I didn't really lie about him, I just avoided being on the spot. It saved a lot of lectures. I saw him every day anyway. I just didn't let them find out. Eventually we broke up, but when we were together it was a real pain to hide it from everyone in my house."

Neither June nor Amy is a juvenile delinquent. Their actions are less a desire to rebel against their parent's authority than a wish to preserve their overwhelming love interest.

This doesn't mean your only recourse, if you find yourself at odds with your teen over their choice of lovers, is to wring your hands and conceal your dissatisfaction. But you have to try tactics other than a show of power. Set limits on the amount of time they spend together or on the phone. Allow them to have the person in your home on a prearranged, agreed-upon schedule. Discuss with your teen the parameters you are setting. Listen to their point of view. Compromise where you can. Be reasonable, but firm. It's far better to show support for your teens even though you can't give them carte blanche approval for their choice.

Now, none of this advice on how to handle the love of your teen's life applies if you suspect, or you know, that the other person is on drugs or gets into trouble with public or school authorities. In that case, you'll have to take another tack. You owe it to your teen to help them see the possible serious negative consequences of continuing that relationship. But, believe me, you can't do it alone. I recommend a counselor.

MR./MS. RIGHT

Usually you will like the person your son or daughter is "mad" about. You may even continue a friendship long after the romantic attraction has faded between them and your teens. I still see several of my kids' one-time loves from time to time when they stop over to say hello. They became part of the family and still are. I liked them so much that I still keep track of them—who is living where, working at what, gotten married, etc. One of my favorite Trivial Pursuit players is a guy in his late twenties I've known since he was in high school. I might have missed knowing him (and winning when he's on my team) if not for my daughter's relationship with him years ago!

Teens, on the whole, use good judgment about selecting someone who is a good person. And they *can* have the ability to spot the difference between infatuation and a relationship that counts. Take, for example, the experience of Anne, age 16: "When Danny came to work at the ice cream place where I work I nearly died. My eyes popped out of my sockets, he was the *best*-looking guy I had ever seen—it was bong, zowie. But now that I've gotten to know him (we've been going out for two months and work the same shift at the store) I see that he's not the 'perfect God' I thought he was. I still think he is great-looking, but he's not up on a pedestal. We get along real well, and who knows maybe we'll be going together for a long time." So, mostly, you can relax, and enjoy how much your teen is learning to experience being in love. Were we ever really *that* young?

A SUMMARY ABOUT LOVE

There really isn't much research information on love in general, or on teenage love in particular. The best I can offer are selected opinions and observations:

- Many people consider "intimacy" to be a better descriptor than the word *love* because it is a more realistic reflection of what occurs in relationships: It reflects that body, mind, and emotions are all crucially involved. The five primary components usually mentioned as essential to achieving intimacy are choice, mutuality, reciprocity, trust, and delight.
- Abraham Maslow describes love as feelings of tenderness and affection for another person, accompanied by great excitement, elation, and even ecstasy. The lovers feel a uniquely enhanced vitality and intensity in everyday life, leading them to a more productive, active involvement in other spheres of their lives.
- Sigmund Freud thought of love as aim-inhibited sex; that is, the original urge for being with another is sexual desire. To him, then, love is the psychological outcome of the cultural thwarting of a biological intention.
- According to psychologist Stanley Schacter, love is a matter of physiological arousal interpreted in a certain way. Sexual arousal—complete with pounding heart, sweaty palms, and heavy breathing—can be easily interpreted (or misinterpreted) as love.
- Masters, Johnson, and Kolodny note that love may have some biological bases, as shown by evolutionary evidence and the interaction between physiological arousal states and emotions, but that love is most importantly a psychosocial phenomenon.
- David Shope, author of *Interpersonal Sexuality*, says: "Love stems from the sensuous need to be near others, to

be touched and to experience this touch as psychologically satisfying. Love grows out of a biological need, sensuousness, and is differentiated in awareness from sexuality because of social conditioning."

• According to any number of researchers and observers, whatever form romantic love takes, it is usually a passing phase, lasting an average of two years.

• Nena O'Neill and George O'Neill, in their book *Open Marriage*, state that, for love to endure, individuality must be maintained. Although each person is nourished by the warmth and acceptance of the other, each must preserve independence and encourage it in the other, so that the potentials of each can develop.

• There is a consensus among the love commentators that it is folly to assume that the path of love is ever smooth and blissful once commitment is made. On the contrary, commitment lurches through sharing, arguing, power grabbing, accusing, reassuring, needing, excluding, explaining, and being vulnerable to prolonged intimacy. The ultimate success or failure of a relationship depends upon whether there is more pleasure than displeasure in the commitment, for certainly there will be both.

To close, here are two of my favorite quotes. The first, a witty, lofty one, by Sir Hugh Walpole:

The most wonderful of all things in life, I believe, is the discovery of another human being with whom one's relationship has a glowing depth, beauty and joy, as the years increase. This inner progressiveness of love between two human beings is a most marvelous thing, it cannot be found by looking for it or by passionately wishing for it. It is a sort of Divine Accident."

And a very earthy one, from a bit of dialogue about love between Lady Chatterley and her lover, Mellors, from *Lady Chatterley's Lover*, by D. H. Lawrence:

"But what do you believe in?" she insisted.
"I don't know."
"Nothing, like all the men I've ever known," she said.
They were both silent. Then he roused himself and said: "Yes, I do believe in something. I believe in being warm-hearted. I believe especially in being warm-hearted in love, in fucking with a warm heart. I believe if men could fuck with warm hearts, and the women take it warm-heartedly everything would come out all right. It's all this cold-hearted fucking that is death and idiocy."

CHAPTER FIVE

WHAT IS SEX? I MEAN REALLY!

SEX IS AN OMNIPRESENT FACT OF TEEN LIFE—a great discovery, a great mess, a great pleasure, a great frustration, and an all-round great muddle. No matter whether they are ready for it or not, it's bound to happen before we're ready for it.

We can't help but wonder how someone who can't make up their mind about what to wear to school can deal with all of the ramifications of having sex. We want our kids to have fulfilling positive sex in their lives, but we don't want them needlessly hurt or, to be blunt, to get pregnant. To boot, we aspire for our son or daughter to deal with themselves and others in an ethical way, to abide by, well, call it morals, as corny as that sounds. But how exactly can we define sexual ethics for them?

THE CROSSWINDS

As kids we were taught that sex before marriage was forbidden fruit (particularly for girls). Then, becoming adults, or as adults, we saw the rule fade away as the Age of Aquarius dawned—people scrambled about doing their own thing, proclaiming, "If it feels good, do it!"

Whether we were activists in the sexual revolution or not, all of us were affected by the shake-up of the traditional order. Indeed, we are a lot more comfortable discussing sex than our parents were. And we no longer fret about the "rights and wrongs" of premarital sex; it is a moot issue, a matter of individual choice. But now, as we watch our kids sexually maturing, we find ourselves thinking about the "shoulds" and "shouldn'ts" all over again. What about *our* kids and "pre-adulthood" sex? Ellen Goodman, a syndicated columnist for the *Boston Globe*, pinpoints the dilemma: "Our agenda is a complicated one, because we do not want to be the new guardians of sexual repression. Nor are we willing to define sexual freedom as the children's right to 'do it.' We are equally uncomfortable with notions that Sex is Evil and Sex is Groovy."

Caught in the crosswinds, it is difficult to communicate clear messages about sexual values, because, in general, we are still assessing the benefit-to-cost ratio of the sexual revolution and, in the specific, we are still evolving our own sexual roles and rules. Our timidity leaves us floundering about defining sexual propriety in the murky "depending upon" context of situational ethics. A code of sexual behavior is made up as we go along, stockpiled with "ifs"—if you know what you are doing, if you use birth control, if you don't get a sexually transmitted disease, if you think it is right for you. Yet teens have only a vague idea of how to deal with these ambiguous guidelines, or they interpret it as a mixed bag, a wishy-washy permission to have sex laden with disapproval. One 16-year-old, commenting on the "if" list, said parents and teachers really mean: "If you do it, don't let me know about it."

AN HONEST DIALOGUE

Okay, we can all agree that the issue of teenage sex is a wary zigzag through a minefield of sexual decisions. But where do we go from here? Many of the people in the field of adolescent sexuality are beginning to look at the value of considering age distinctions as a positive way to engage in a realistic dialogue with teens. There are sex educators who say the essential message should be "no teenage sex," but there is a growing consensus among educators and counselors that dictating "no teenage sex" is mostly wishful thinking. For example, Carol Gilligan, associate professor of education at Harvard, says, "We have to say that it may be fine to have sex at 18, but 14 is too young." Elizabeth Roberts, author of *Childhood Sexual Learning*, also opts for making age distinctions for teenage sexual standards: "I just think we have to make some rules again, like 13 is too young. Period." Personally, I believe teens under 16 are simply too young to handle the emotional and physical consequences of sex, and need to hear that message loud and clear.

Most parents know it is futile to pin their hope on the possibility that young people won't experiment with sex until the last rose has faded on the senior prom corsage. Parents tell me they are more able to accept, even if they can't wholeheartedly approve, their teen having a sexual relationship at age 17 or 18, because, at this age, sons and daughters are more apt to be able to make good decisions. Not so mysteriously, by this time our teens see themselves as almost adults, and are either graduating from high school and going off to college, or moving out to apartments and working.

This idea of accepting, or at least tolerating, certain kinds of privilege or behavior based upon reaching a certain age isn't really new. As a society, we have many age-distinction rules—there are legal ages to reach before you can get a driver's license, vote, drink, marry. I'm not lobbying for a legal "sexual coming of age." I am seeking a better way to deal with the fact that many young people will not wait until they are married to have sex or wait until they have reached the age of majority. Forming an informal cultural norm that under a certain age, say, 17, having sex is "too soon" and not appropriate, may be the most realistic way to set some much-needed limits, and the most logical replacement for the outmoded traditional rule "no sex before marriage" that teenagers ignore or rebel against. Remember, teens aren't the sexual revolutionists. They didn't initiate it; they inherited it from us.

Considering an age of consent doesn't mean parents hand over the keys to the house to their post-17 teen to "have sex" or make arrangements at the local motel for them to celebrate a specific birthday. It simply means *having a dialogue with teens about postponing sex until they are mature enough to make decisions that will lead them into a positive sexual experience, rather than into ones that are disappointing or, even worse, destructive.* And for many teens, this may mean postponing sex until they are out of high school for any number of good reasons (more about those later on in this chapter). All and all, I think encouraging them to think before they act, to consider the merits of saying "Not now" to sex, is healthier and more on target than the rigid rule "Say no to sex." Our goal isn't to make them negative about sex, but to use good judgment and not to be pressured into something before they are ready. Give them a lot of support for being cautious about sex.

One of the biggest problems you will face is trying to help your teen have a sense of when they are mature enough to make a decision about having a sexual relationship. There isn't any magical surge of maturity on one particular birthday. The point isn't that you pick an age when they will have your tacit if not explicit acceptance of their decision to have sex, but rather that you want them to know that under a certain age (whatever you think that age is) you can't sanction them having sex. It is critically important to discuss this "when" as also being contingent upon their having developed a personal sense of self-esteem and ability to communicate with another person about this person's as well as their own intimacy needs and feelings, and they should also be ready to be responsible about contraception.

I also suggest two parallel strategies. One is to talk about masturbation as a way to relieve sexual tension. It's not harmful, and is a good way to understand how the body responds sexually. In fact, masturbation is also called "self-pleasuring." Convey to them that "touching" yourself is very natural and *nothing* to feel guilty about. I know this is a particularly unsettling topic for many people because of all the negative messages surrounding masturbation, but those "nasty" ideas about it are better laid to rest once and for all.

Another is to talk to them about the options other than intercourse that people have to express sexual feelings: necking, petting, or what sex educators call "sexual fondling." Teens are needlessly disparaging of sexual play that can relieve sexual tensions without "going all the way."

Assessing the tendency toward premature sexual intercourse among teenagers, Robert Sorenson, researcher and author of *Adolescent Sexuality in Contemporary America*, poses this question: "What if our culture were to encourage beginning sexual activities among those who are intimately involved with one another, and propose that they stay with this early sexual phase?" He goes on to explain why he thinks this is a tactic worth considering: "Most adolescents are giving themselves little time for beginning sexual activities and move directly to sexual intercourse. One reason for this may be that in our society sexual intercourse is widely considered the only valid expression of sexual love. Another reason may be the unwillingness of many parents to consider sexual beginning activities as totally different from sexual intercourse." In other words, we tend to diminish the value of the prologue and overemphasize the main event.

Let your teen know they have a lot to gain by not rushing it. They need to hear (passé though it may be) that sexual petting or fondling is a better learning experience than sprinting in a mad dash to intercourse. They can discover much about their own sexuality and become better skilled at handling their sexual feelings as well as those of another person.

Explain to your son or daughter that having sex haphazardly, or as an obligation, ends badly. That's one of the reasons why sexual problems are as widespread as the common cold. Unless sex takes place in a time and place where you feel comfortable and with someone you like, trust, and can talk to, it can be an empty, frustrating experience. As so aptly described by that old wag Lord Chesterfield: "The enjoyment is quite temporary. The cost is exorbitant and the position is simply ridiculous."

Keep in mind that, no matter what adults think, teens don't have to have our permission to have sex. They may plan it or blunder into it, and we can't do more than give some guidance on how to make that decision. But isn't it reassuring to know that teens who feel they can openly talk to their parents about sexual feelings, and the real world of teenage sexual pressures, are generally more discriminating about their sexual activity? They are more likely to postpone sex, to have a caring relationship with their partner when they do have sex, and to be more consistent about using contraception.

OTHER VOICES

Above all you have to contend with the fact that you aren't the only influence on your teenager's ideas about sex. Most teens learn about reproduction from school, but hear about masturbation, homosexuality, and sexual intercourse from friends, which means a teen's friends have a strong impact on their understanding of sexuality and on their sexual activity. Teens tell me there is a lot of pressure to have sex from their friends who are involved in a sexual relationship. "Being a virgin means you are teased by your friends as 'chicken'; you feel like an oddball," says Amelia, age 15. I could recite for you any number of statements that sound like Amelia's. And you may be surprised to know that many of these are from young boys. After a talk at a high school, a boy (ninth-grader), with fine blond hair and a clear rosy complexion, shyly asked me if he could ask me something "real personal." We went to a quiet corner of the auditorium and he explained his problem: "I really like a girl a lot, and I don't want to lose her, but she wants me to have sex with her, and I don't want to have sex. She says if I don't, she'll drop me because it's embarrassing to go around with a virgin."

Many teens have sex because they are in love and want to express those feelings in an intimate way (just as adults do). Sadly, many have sex not because they are feeling loving, or even lustful, but because they are under a lot of pressure to fit in with the crowd. Thus, for many teens, having sex for the first time may be a way of achieving membership in the peer culture.

IS EVERYBODY REALLY DOING IT?

In trying to understand young people's sexual behavior, it's best to come to terms with the extent to which teenage sex can be a contemporary declaration of independence. Forming sexual relationships involves risk-taking, trying out new experiences, and being tuned in to other people. Having a sexual relationship, for some teens, is a personal resource they mobilize to become whole and feeling persons. Others want to have sex because they see it as a milestone, an experience from which "maturity" will ensue.

All you can do as a parent is to put the peer pressure on your son and daughter into perspective for them.

Bring out the fact it's really a myth that "everybody is doing it." After all, if by age 15 about one girl in five is not a virgin, four out of five are. And if by age 17 about 50 percent of girls have had sex, 50 percent haven't. For boys, I admit this point gets a little thin. Still, some studies report that by age 15 only about 40 percent of boys have had sex. I'm not suggesting you gloss over the reality that by the end of the teen years a vast majority of teens have had sex at least once: 80 percent of boys, 70 percent of girls. But that doesn't mean all teens are "sexually active." Some teens have had intercourse once or twice. Some had sex at age 15 and not again until they were 18. Help them see the potential harm for them, as an individual, of doing something they aren't ready for, or don't really want to do.

Don't downplay their need to belong to the group, but point out that sex isn't a spectator sport. Having sex, or not having sex, is a personal decision and takes place in private.

And personal, private matters aren't something they have to reveal for public scrutiny. If they want to wait, tell them (a takeoff on an old song) that it's nobody's business but their own. That's how several teens have told me they deal with the pressure. For example, Joyce, age 14, says, "When someone asks me if I am a virgin, I look 'em straight in the eye and tell them to bug off, or ask them, 'What's it to you?' " A sense of assertiveness can provide some backbone for your son or daughter to withstand the onslaught of questions and teasing.

But whether they wait until they are past adolescence to have intercourse or they don't, young people have sexual feelings and they are very personal. Don't confuse sexuality with "sexactuality": Teens are sexual long before they have sex. And when it comes to the decision to have sex, you can't make it for them. You have to let go of that part of your almost-adult child, which no longer belongs to you.

SEXUAL STIRRINGS

Teens respond to their emerging sexuality through a complicated mix of emotional and physical longings. They wonder about the "force" of sex: what propels people to have sex, and then what really happens. They fantasize about sex, forming images that fluctuate between gossamer-veiled, slow-motion romantic setting and a wildly lusty orgy. Although having fantasies is perfectly normal, young people worry that their thoughts are bizarre or perverted and that, because they have them, they are abnormal. They worry if, when they do have sex, they'll be able to do it right, or if they will make fools of themselves.

They have surmised people have sex for any number of reasons, not all of them because they want to make love. For example, here is a sampling of what a group of high school students told me are the reasons they think teenagers have sex:

for fun
to get it over with
to fit in with the crowd
curiosity
to avoid breaking up
as a way of getting love
for money
can't control themselves any longer
it feels good
everyone else is doing it
it makes them feel great
they are mentally and socially ready to share their body with someone
why not?

Some of this suggests a factor that grown-ups frequently overlook. Sexual intercourse, to many young people—despite the ambivalence, the imprudence, the flamboyance, the need to *épater les bourgeois* (astonish the bourgeois)—is simply a lot of pleasure. Don't get so serious about discussing sex with your son or daughter that you stifle communicating what makes it worth doing. Physical pleasure, skin on skin, touching, embracing—with an earthiness and humanity to go with them—are playfully enjoyable.

SEX, ITS OWN SELF

What can you tell your teen about sex? The truth. Good sex gives a person a feeling of well-being that is unlike anything else; it is one of the most powerful, pleasing human desires. Admit that people can enjoy sex for its own sake even if most people say sex is more pleasurable and rewarding within a caring and trusting relationship.

First and foremost, impart to your teen the positive side of being sexual. We are all sexual the day we are born; sexuality is an integral part of our lives, an enhancement and enrichment of our total personality.

Because teens get so many messages to the contrary, convey to them that sex isn't an "act." You don't commit it, you experience it with another person. You don't give it or take it, you share it. You'll find a ready audience because most teens, especially those beyond the early stage of adolescence, are less concerned with the occurrence of sexual intercourse than with its context. State that a sexual relationship is basically a sexual friendship. It may be very intimate, not very intimate, or something in between, depending on the symbolic meanings each of the persons involved attaches to the relationship.

Don't isolate sex as a separate part of a relationship, or not connected to a relationship. Roger Libby, a noted sex educator, takes this point further: "To look at sex as a separate segment of a relationship or to ferret it out of the total relationship as something totally different from other ways of relating distorts reality. It puts conceptual blinders on us so that we cannot see what is happening, what is the meaning of the experience, what are the motives and the consequences."

IT'S NO MYSTERY

Teens have gleaned—from reading any sex manuals they can get their hands on, or from their friends—the basic mechanics of sex: Sexual intercourse is when an erect penis enters the vagina. But they are naive about sexual chemistry—that marvelous combination of psychological and biological impulses that results in sexual attraction and desire.

Without being too technical and at the risk of being a bit simplistic, tell them that sexual desire is a response, felt by the whole body, triggered by a stimulus, to a person who is sexually appealing. Attraction is easier to recognize than describe. Philosophers, artists, writers, and just about everyone else have struggled to isolate what it is about another person that attracts us to them and vice versa, to no avail. In essence, I'm convinced it's the gestalt that counts. Sexual attraction makes us desire to know that person better, be physically close to them.

Teens need to know that, while being sexually attracted to someone is normal and natural, going beyond that point to having sex doesn't "just happen." Sexual desire and intercourse follow a pattern of cycles, beginning with sexual arousal and climaxing in orgasm. When we are attracted to someone and are physically stimulated by kissing and petting, our hypothalamus (that bundle of tissue at the base of our brain), acting through the long-distance messenger of the pituitary gland, modulates our blood pressure, temperature, and breathing rate. This combined hormonal activity produces a strong feeling of sexual excitement. The male's penis engorges with blood and becomes erect. A woman's breasts become sensitive and slightly enlarged, and her vagina moist. If arousal gets more intense, nerve impulses race back and upward, to spine, to brain, to hypothalamus. Muscles stiffen, hearts beat faster, even the pupils of the eyes slightly dilate. The muscles of the penis contract, nerve impulses rush to the brain, and the male climaxes and ejaculates. The woman's body becomes more tense, her clitoris withdraws, contractions ripple along the walls of her vagina, and she experiences a feeling of relief: orgasm. For both men and women, the heartbeat now slows, and blood pressure drops. It's difficult to describe orgasm, because it is an individual experience. Generally people say that it is an intense feeling of sexual pleasure or tension followed by a calm feeling. It's rare for both partners to climax at the same time. And not all women have an orgasm every time. There are any number of reasons why: They weren't aroused enough, they felt pressured, or they weren't comfortable with this partner or about sex in that place or at that time. Men apparently have less difficulty in reaching a climax.

I grant you that describing sexual intercourse in this Masters and Johnson milieu (excitement, plateau, orgasm, resolution) might not be the most romantic of definitions, but at least it's factual. Some people fear that giving young people such a "scientific" description of a very human experience will distract from its value and enjoyment. I don't think so; Galileo's scientific analysis of the universe did not destroy our sense of wonder when we gaze up at a starry night.

Once teenagers understand that sex isn't something centered only in the genitals, they will be better able to recognize how the feeling of being sexually excited, "turned on," is the catalyst leading to sexual intercourse. Let your son or daughter know that sexual arousal is powerful stuff. A person may not be planning to become aroused, but with enough kissing and fondling control switches from the reasoning forebrain to the lower brain and the autonomic nervous system, and seeking to become sexually satisfied becomes a strong impulse. Now, tell them that being sexually excited doesn't mean the body shifts to automatic pilot. There are many places along the way to sexual climax where the brakes can be put on.

Teens need to appreciate the fact that being sexually attracted to a person is a grand feeling just as it is. Remind them that sexual excitement in itself is very wonderful. Those feelings don't necessarily have to lead to sexual intercourse. But don't overemphasize the intrinsic power of self-control. The fact of the matter is that, once a person is intensely sexually aroused, it is difficult to be rational about what is going on. After all, people are only human. Therefore, communicate to your son or daughter the importance of knowing one's limits. If a person doesn't want to have sexual intercourse—for whatever the reason—they need to think twice before becoming involved in a heavy-duty petting situation. Or they need to decide in advance, and communicate to the other person involved, that sexual fondling is where they will draw the line.

While young people themselves concede that they make mistakes in the expression of their sexuality (who is immune from that?), the majority don't believe in sex for physical reasons alone and disapprove of people using other people sexually. Most teenagers are concerned that sex be honest, and agree with the basic tenet that a sexual relationship is foremost something that matters. A vast majority of teens, much like most adults, practice serial monogamy. They may have relationships that include sex, but only one at a time. It might help you to know that what young people seek is what grown-ups seek: a loving and affectionate relationship, not just sex per se.

OTHER RULES, OTHER VALUES

Once again, let me put up a warning sign. Raising your daughter or son to have a positive, healthy attitude about sexuality means you will be in sharp contrast to the well-entrenched notions that sex is distasteful at best, an occasion of sin at worst. The message to postpone sex based on personal ethical decisions is a far cry from what they will hear from every other corner of our society. And just because you wouldn't heap a ration of guilt and shame about "premarital" sex on your teen doesn't mean others won't. Our kids live in a world in which, despite the kaleidoscopic sexual environment, the dominant cultural norm is still one of anxiety and fear. A parent of a 15-year-old daughter and a 13-year-old son told me she never told them sex was disgusting or immoral. Now, she wonders, "After letting my daughter grow up uninhibited about sex, I'm worried she'll get a bad reputation or be misled by boys who have been taught to view girls as sex objects. As for my son, he may be sexually open but I'm afraid he will be misjudged by others, and I'm concerned about him having to play games with girls who can't be honest about sex." This parent's concerns are judicious.

While the majority of adults and teens, even if they don't act on it, don't believe in the traditional church-societal rule that "sex is to be only partaken within the bonds of marriage," there are still a number of people who do. Among your son's or daughter's peers there are bound to be some who feel that sex before marriage is a sin, and view people who think differently about the subject as sinners, not decent folk. Sadly, some of these young people taught to believe that premarital sex is the sure route to hell don't abstain. And because their actions don't match their beliefs, they often carry a tremendous burden of guilt, which can be passed on to your teen. Greg's experience sheds light on how this takes place. He says, "I was going with someone last year I really liked. One thing led to another and one day we had sex. She said she wanted to as much as I did. But afterward, all she did was cry that she was going to hell and it was my fault. I felt like a creep. Lower than low-down. I couldn't face her at school so I didn't go to classes for three days, and I nearly busted a test in civics."

Some people would like to return to the days when "fornication" was illegal. Says Noreen Barr, legislative director of Phyllis Schlafly's Eagle Forum, "I'd like to outlaw premarital sex," but admits "there's an enforcement problem—invasion of privacy. But I see no problem with having it on the books." As absurd and out-of-sync as this sounds, the minority make a lot of noise and have appointed themselves as the moral guardians of us all. This group of people may rarely interact with you in your world, but teenagers, including yours, because they are under the auspices of school authorities, bear the brunt of their missionary zeal. Check out the average high school curriculum: There is a near-worship of "family" complete with stereotypical sex roles for men and women (breadwinner, breadbaker); women in the work force are considered a "problem"; and overall there is a queasy tight-lipped silence about the joys of sex. In most communities, these groups have made sex education "controversial," put down "women's lib," and work untiringly to ban hundreds of books that dare to mention sex.

The actions of these groups opposed to enlightening young people about sexuality are something to behold. Recently, after I spoke to several high school classes in a charming city in the Northwest, shock waves of protest from a small but very indignant group of parents hit the local newspaper's Letters to the Editor and the school board. Why? I used the words *pubic hair* and I didn't honor female virgins as being on a higher plane than nonvirgins, and I did not preach chastity before marriage. I said many of the same things I say in this book: It's better for teens to postpone having sex, not to be sexually exploitive, to be aware of the emotional and physical consequences of having sex, and to make good personal sexual decisions. Still, among other things, I was called "immoral" and "obscene," and was accused of destroying the moral fiber of young people.

Clearly you want your teen to respect the value systems

of others, but this doesn't mean they have to buckle under to the piousness of the traditional moralists. The best way to equip your son or daughter to deal with those who view sex through the lenses of guilt, sin, and punishment is to give them some insight about both the "liberal" and "conservative" tacks. If they don't know the rationale and values inherent in different standards, they will be vulnerable to being sexually exploited by others—hedonists, puritans, or any mixture of the two.

A BRIEF REVIEW OF "TRADITION"

Inform your teen that traditional sexual mores of valuing (and demanding) female virginity are historically linked to a slew of socioeconomic conditions and propagated by the teachings of many religions. A woman's reproductive capacity was valued because large families were valued. Among the landed gentry, marriage was the only avenue of social and economic security for women. A father, looking to make a good deal on the marriage of his daughter, had to accept a much lower bride price if she wasn't a certified virgin. Patriarchy was the system of inheritance, and a virgin bride was the assurance the man would not be tricked into raising another's man's child and that the rights of inheritance would not be challenged by another "tribe." When arranged marriages went out with the Model-T, the insidious Good Girl/Bad Girl categorizing of women formed social pressure on women to remain "innocent" to protect the patriarchal order.

After you have given your teen some insight into the roots of our sexual mores, it is a good idea to admit that, once, it might have been a useful system to ensure the welfare of children. Illegitimate births often relegated a child to a life of neglect. However, what is useful at some point in history has to be adjusted in the light of inventions, technology, and changes in social and economic conditions. With effective contraception there no longer is any rationale to justify sexual constraints on women, be that in the bedroom or anyplace else. And with an economic system that doesn't hinge on male inheritance, men no longer have to be burdened with safeguarding their tribal riches, or of being the sole provider for their families.

BOYS WILL BE BOYS?

What has all of this information about the link between patriarchy and traditionally different sexual standards for males and females to do with your teen? In three weighty words: the double standard. Our tendency is to ignore it in the misguided belief that it faded from collective memory sometime or another in the last ten years. Well, it didn't. That's not to say that the double standard exists as it did in its heyday of the fifties and early sixties. There is a lot less hypocrisy; times have changed, but in uneven ways. A decade of Phil Donahue has not made most teenage guys any more sensitive to girls' feelings. Sex between many teens is mostly something boys get and girls give, but now girls who say "no" feel compelled to say why. The single standard may be forthcoming, but it has hardly arrived in the hallowed halls of high schools.

You can't wave a magic wand and make the double standard disappear for them. You can make a valiant effort to challenge it. However, before you tilt at that particular windmill, you need to be aware of how it currently operates among teens.

While sex is increasingly more permissible for girls, permission is conditional. And the new conditions sound a lot like a page taken from the same old double-standard rule-book. Although it isn't as flagrant as it used to be, girls are still separated into two camps depending on their sexual activity. Girls judged as "too easy" about sex get tagged "sleazy." Girls worthy of dating are "not sleazy." The term "Good Girl" has been relegated to museums, but the concept can be heard loud and clear when talking to teens. When I ask teenagers how a girl can avoid being tagged "sleazy," I find consensus: having sex only with the guy they are going with, or being madly in love with a guy (the latter if it happens once).

In addition to the conditions imposed on the reasons a girl has sex, there is a judgment made on how soon she has sex. Explains Michael, age 18, "If she goes to bed right away with a guy, at a party or on a first date, she is probably a sleaze. A girl can get a bad reputation if she steps out of an ongoing relationship and dates around a lot." He thought a minute, and then came out with this provoking question: "Don't you think a lot of girls use the double standard to establish a pecking order?" Then he added, "Girls are harsh judges of each other and gossip as much as guys. They never try to defend another girl. I've heard them say, 'She's just a sleaze,' and really run her down."

Don't be too quick to dismiss his observation because it isn't what we want to hear, or because it sounds so, well, unseemly. He has a point. If you are female, be honest. Remember the high school "trashings" and how girls were cut from the herd if they made even the slightest departure from the group's ideas or if the group thought they might taint the rest of its members with a "bad" reputation? And all we had to do was to "hear" about her possible misstep because we didn't require any evidence? Recall how much we loved to gossip about other girls, talking about who was "cheap" and who might be, and how critical we were? Well, how much do you think has changed? Listen in on the conversation when a group of girls are hanging out and I'll bet you will hear some of the same kind of juicy gossiping with the word "sleazy" substituted for "bad" or "cheap" or whatever.

LUCKY STUDS

I've asked teens, "What about guys? Can they get a 'bad' reputation? Can they be labeled sleazy?" The response is a ripple of chuckles and wave after wave of self-conscious shrugs. So I persevere: "What would you call a guy who has sex with several different girls?" The answer (usually smugly offered by the guys): "A stud," or "Lucky."

However, most of girls didn't respond so quickly or easily. Take, for example, Janet, age 15, who was adamant that a guy could "get a bad reputation if it's known he has slept with a lot of girls." I asked her what he would be labeled. After thinking this through a minute, with a deep furrowing of the brow, she responded: "He'd be called a 'lover-boy,' or 'fast.' " I pursued that point with her, and a group of her friends who were gathered around us with keen interest, by posing a question to all of them: "Do these labels have the same meaning as 'sleazy'?" After a lot of chatter among members of the group they reluctantly came to a conclusion (the same one as all of the teen groups I surveyed): "Well, not really."

CONFLICTING REASONS

Why should we be so concerned about the effect of the double standard? Don't kids eventually grow out of believing in it? Is it somehow connected to adolescence? Maybe, but we all pay a price as a teenager, and as an adult, that is not worth paying. These very different sexual rules for boys and girls produce different social pressures, which in turn result in different, and opposite, expectations of sex. Males push toward greater physical intimacy and are willing to bargain with love and affection, while females push toward greater commitment and are willing to exchange sex in return for promises of love.

Explain to your teen that one of the reasons you aren't an advocate of the double standard is that it is emotionally harmful to both genders. Take, for instance, the experience of Kim, age 15: "I went out with this guy I really liked. After two weeks of us going together, I slept with him. The *next day* he told me he was in love with another girl. I thought I'd die. How could he be in love with someone else? I was sure he loved me; he even told me he did." This kind of story was repeated to me in several variations in every state I traveled to. And, every time, my heart broke a little.

Point out that guys are not immune to getting hurt. The notion that guys are "sexual warriors" means that his ego is in for a shellacking if sex wasn't all it was advertised to be. Or if he isn't prone to being sexually aggressive he can get put down as a wimp. Steven, age 16, told me of his experience: "Why are guys expected to make all the moves? I never know if I should persist or desist. I can't read minds. A girl I really was stuck on dropped me like a hot potato just because I didn't hit on her. It got around school that I was a sexual retard and everyone teases me. You know, Steve, the Great Wimpola."

Besides scarring your teen emotionally, the double standard begets the worst kind of sexual ethics. Boys get pressured into having to prove their manhood through sexual exploits, and develop a knack for braggadocio instead of honesty. It can be a devastating blow to a girl's self-esteem and ability to form a trusting relationship. Says Janet, age 17, "I've gotten a lousy reputation for sleeping around. It isn't fair. I only had sex with two guys, and I was going with each of them when it happened. Now when I date a guy he expects to have sex—'You did it before.' I'm so miserable I'm trying to go to another high school next year, but my parents don't understand why, and I can't tell them."

Because girls bear the brunt of pregnancy, we, as parents (consciously and unconsciously), find ourselves setting more limits on daughters than we do on sons—curfew at earlier hours, scrutinizing how they spend their time, playing detective about their relationships. Beyond the very real worry "she could get pregnant," there is the possibility of a daughter, given the double-standard operative, acquiring a "bad reputation," which we worry could become a self-fulfilling prophecy. So it's understandable for a parent to feel more uneasy about a daughter's sexual involvement (potential or actual) than a son's. But that uneasiness may lead to unwittingly setting up girls to make bad sexual decisions.

Girls overly protected don't fare very well in the rough and tumble of teen sexual relationships. "Good Girls" are ill-equipped to deal with their sexual feelings. To protect themselves from losing the boy, or their reputation, girls convince themselves they are making love, not having sex. The denial of being sexual leads them to not be responsible for their own emotions and behavior.

Although Cyndi Lauper may sing the song "Girls Just Want to Have Fun," fun is one thing they definitely are not having. As Lesley Jane Nonkin learned from survey interviews with hundreds of teenage girls, girls just want to belong. She found "the girls' misinformation and tragic insecurity very upsetting." Their sexual "sophistication" gleaned from TV sex and their notions of sexual freedom have not eliminated this tried-and-true line: "If you really loved me, you'd sleep with me." Nor has it made it any easier for a girl to spot it as such. Nonkin adds, "It's as if the women's movement never happened. To be a female today is not to be liberated, it is to be willing to be told, and used." Her observation, among other things, was based on how girls answered one of the questions: "Are you a virgin?" Several girls answered yes, then crossed it out and marked no. Just as many wrote no and crossed it out to answer yes. One girl was so ambivalent about her experience that she told Nonkin she was so drunk that night she "couldn't remember": that way she could have it both ways.

MAKING A DENT

We have an alternative. Teach your daughter about her own special worth as a person, and support her in her struggle to overcome the lingering sexual constraints placed on women.

Announce to your son and daughter that the double standard is blatantly ridiculous. What is right for girls is right for boys. We are all born virgins. Sooner or later, out of love, sexual pressure, or plain curiosity, most of us have sex with another person, and are immediately disqualified as virgins. What has "good" got to do with it? And ask what is the fuss about girls "losing their virginity"? How can she possibly lose something that requires deliberate action by two people?

Examine with them one of the rationales underlying sexual double standards: A man *should* be more sexually experienced than a woman. Supposedly that makes for a happier marriage. Apart from being totally off base on the inner workings of a happy marriage, it's also a mathematical impossibility. Discuss the obvious: It takes practice to become experienced, and it takes two to practice. Besides, the sex drive is comparable for both sexes.

FACTS FOR SONS

Expect as much from sons as from daughters. Emphasize to your son that you want him to be caring and responsible toward his partner. Letty Cottin Pogrebin, writing about the need to combat the double standard by giving teens new messages, says: "For your son, who is growing alongside girls who will expect equality in the bedroom as well as the boardroom, the new sexual ideology affirms that 'scoring' is stealing unless the girl is as willing, as risk-free, and as sexually satisfied as he is." Then, be sure to get across to him the message that it's not the girl's responsibility to "restrain" a guy, or her "fault" if they go "too far."

Don't hesitate to poke holes in the idea that men put women on a pedestal to show admiration and devotion. Point out that this notion is one way to keep women segregated, it sets them up for a fall, and it's really sexism.

Tell your son that losing respect for girls who have sex, or searing their reputation because they do, signifies contempt for women, not high-toned morality. Now, take a deep breath and tell your daughter all of the above.

MAKING BETTER CHOICES

Teens need to hear that having sex is a choice a person makes, and that each person has to make that decision for themselves. Obviously, they can use some practical advice from you on how to make good choices. As a help to you, I've put together some pointers dealing with sexual decisions from a bounty of good sources, many being teens themselves, as to what a person can consider when in the throes of trying to figure out how sex fits into the context of their lives:

Fairness. Each partner must freely consent. This means

that if one is coerced, either through persuasion ("You would if you loved me"), veiled threats ("If you don't, I'll break up with you"), or physical pressure, it is exploitation. Being fair means not applying any pressure, either psychological or physical.

A confusing part of consent for teens (and a lot of adults) is the assumption that it is the male's role to "talk" the woman into having sex, and that for sex to happen he has to keep up the pressure because, although she acts reluctant, "she wants to." Be firm about the fact that consent must be active not passive, and that each person has the right to say no or change their mind—even at the last minute. Giving in is not consent.

To illustrate how important it is for you to get the point across to your son or daughter that sex must be freely consented to, read the following responses teenage students gave, in a research survey, to the question, "Is it all right if a male holds a female down and forces her to engage in intercourse if . . .":

	Answering Yes	
	FEMALE	MALE
. . . he spent a lot of money on her?	12%	39%
. . . she led him on?	27%	54%
. . . they have dated a long time?	32%	43%
. . . she says she is going to have sex with him then changes her mind?	21%	36%
. . . she has let him touch her above the waist?	28%	39%
. . . she is stoned or drunk?	18%	39%

Source: "Adolescent Cues and Signals: Sex and Assault." Paper presented at the Western Psychological Association Meeting, San Diego, CA, April 1979, by Roseann Giarusso, Paula Johnson, Jacqueline Goodchilds, and Gail Zellman, University of California, Los Angeles.

It makes the hair on the back of your neck stand straight up, doesn't it? The teenage boys' attitudes are bad enough, but look at the percentage of girls who went along with them. No matter how one gilds the lily, all of the conditions given above could be described as "acquaintance rape"—where a rape occurs on a date. (A full discussion of sexual assault is beyond the scope of this book, for more details see reference list.)

It didn't surprise me to read, in a recent survey of sexually active girls 16 and under, that what they wanted the most information on was how to say no without hurting the other person's feelings. Basically girls are uncertain about whether it's okay to say no to unwanted sexual advances, and are unwilling to stand up for the basic right to control their own bodies. There are girls who think—and say—that if a boy pays for dinner he has bought himself at least a kiss.

Honesty. Don't hedge when discussing what you mean by honesty. Lay it out: no exploitation, no manipulation. Reinforce the fact that these shifty moves are not limited to males seducing innocent fair maidens. Sex educator Roger Libby observes, "Adolescent females can be equally exploitative in 'using' sex to commit a boyfriend to an exclusive relationship, or push the partner toward marriage by manipulating the relationship with sexual behavior. The obvious exploitative female move is to purposefully get pregnant, or to feign pregnancy to 'trap' the male into marriage." From my experience with teens, I can say that most teens do not want to exploit others sexually, but many fall into the pattern because it is so prevalent. Some teens tend to use ploys of manipulation because they are not aware that is actually what they are doing.

Enlighten them by explaining how manipulation isn't far removed from exploitation. The line between them often commingles. Define manipulation as having sex with another person under false pretenses. You need to use some specifics, because teens don't always understand exactly what we are trying to get across to them. As one teenage boy said, "My mom tells me I shouldn't take advantage of a girl. But what does that mean?" And as Loni, a 16-year-old, asked, "What does 'using' a guy mean? Is that when you go on a date with someone you sorta like, but not that much; you just want to go to the party or the concert?"

Some examples of manipulation you could use: telling someone you love them when you don't; having sex with someone to get them to go steady with you as a popularity ploy; having sex for your pleasure only; using sex to boost your reputation or as a way to prove your own masculinity or femininity; or saying you must have sex or you will physically suffer (there is yet to be recorded a permanent physical disability from an unresolved case of horniness).

Responsibility. Each partner must be responsible for the other person's feelings as well as their own. And each must take precautions to avoid sexually transmitted diseases and pregnancy.

BENCHMARKS FOR SEXUAL DECISIONS

Once you have covered those vital ethical issues, it's time to move on to considerations involved in deciding how sex fits into one's life. Try to stimulate their thinking about how having sex might affect a relationship they value, and, beyond that, the effect having sex could have on their own personal options and freedom to shape their own life. Reinforce to them the option they have to postpone sex until they can be sure they are sharing the experience with someone they care about and trust, and at a time when they aren't anxious or confused about their and the other person's ability to handle intimacy.

Some benchmarks for sexual decision making you can pass on to your teen:

• Sex doesn't necessarily indicate love, and vice versa. Two people can be physically attracted and sexually satisfy each other, and have very little else in common. It's possible to love someone yet not want to have a sexual relationship. You can love someone but feel that you're not ready (for any number of reasons) to cope with sex. You don't have to have sex with someone because you care for them, or because they love you. A misplaced feeling of social obligation is no substitute for sexual desire. If you have a nagging worry that you shouldn't, or you feel unsure, listen to yourself. If in doubt, don't. You are the best, and only, judge of your own feelings.

• Sex can enhance a good relationship or detract from a loving friendship. Because sex is a very intimate experience, one of life's most personal moments, a person is bound to have a certain amount of emotional vulnerability. A sexual relationship may grab their emotions in ways they aren't ready for and can't wholly anticipate. When a sexually intimate relationship ends, it hurts. And you can't count on being the first to say good-bye. (Rejection is rejection whether you are age 16 or 46, but for teenagers, who are particularly vulnerable, it can cause a serious blow to their fragile self-esteem.)

• There is a tremendous amount of hype about sex. Without an understanding of your own sexuality, and a partner who is similarly secure, sex can be a great letdown. Sex can turn into a failed experiment instead of a satisfying experience because of the tremendous amount of anticipation built up through the propaganda of romantic novels, movies, TV, and magazines. Typical sex hype is sex described as, "Wave after wave of almost unbearable pleasure washed over them both, until each exploded in ecstasy." Real life is seldom as sexually perfect. Great sex doesn't just happen. There's not much you can do to guarantee sex will be a terrific, worthwhile experience, but there is a lot a person can do to stack the odds in their favor.

• Suggest to your son or daughter that they give having a sexual relationship the same kind of constructive attention that they did, or will give, to learning to drive a car. Bumbling into a sexual relationship can leave a person with a nasty aftertaste.

• Impart to them the fact that *fireworks* and *great ecstasy* are not the words most teens use to describe sex. Despite being intensely sexually primed, teens are not only inexperienced, but sadly ignorant about how much time, effort, and being in tune to the other person are required to mutually enjoy lovemaking and having sex. Sex (among teens) is almost always hurried, uncomfortable, and disappointing. This applies more to girls, because they almost never have an orgasm. Guys, because they are supposed to know what to do and really don't, suffer from a lot of performance anxiety. Because they often fail to maintain an erection, or ejaculate immediately when the penis enters the vagina, boys can feel sexually inadequate. And this type of experience doesn't do much for their self-confidence. All in all, the most common aftermath felt by teens is what researcher David Weiss tags The Peggy Lee Syndrome: "Is that all there is?"

• Having sex has a way of taking over a teenage relationship. It can put a lot of personal and social pressure on one or both of the partners. Once a couple enters into a sexual relationship, the uncertainty and worry about "Is it me or is it sex?"; "Will it last?"; "What would my parents think?"; or "What if she gets pregnant?" begin. And then there is sexual jealousy to deal with, and it can be a heavy burden because each is expected to cleave exclusively to each other at the stage of their life when they want to explore the edge of the envelope. It's perfectly natural to be attracted to a lot of different people, but most teens can't handle their sexual partner showing even a friendly interest in another person.

• Many teenagers say that after they began having sex everything went sour in the relationship. Becoming involved in a one-on-one relationship kept them in a Noah's Ark mode. Being a couple put a damper on hanging out with other people and having time to do what they want to. Teenage girls complain about having less time for their girlfriends, studying, being involved in school activities, and going places with their families; they feel cut off from the rest of their world. Some say dating isn't fun anymore, because going to the movies or dances gets shortchanged: "He doesn't want to do anything anymore but go someplace and have sex." Guys say the pressure to be committed to the girl—by her, his friends, her friends—forces them to continue a relationship they would rather end, or makes them feel more obligated to the girl than they would like to be. Said Gene, age 17, "You can get stuck. Everyone knows you are a 'couple,' and if you try to break it up with her so you can date someone else, everyone gets on your case."

In a nutshell, given the tight parameters that surround teenage sexual relationships, they can stunt opportunities to meet and know other people, and hinder the freedom to explore who you really are, and what you really want. Or, as one savvy teenage critic put it, "It can be a real drag."

A LAST WORD

To sum up what we can say to our teens about sexual ethics and responsibility, I really like what Mary S. Calderone, the eminent sex educator, told a group of young people: "At the present time the best we adults can do is to set some rules and expect you to obey them; give you as much factual information as we possibly can; and last, but not least, *place on the record our conviction that sex should never be casual or accidental, but should be the result of the conscious decision of two people*, mutually arrived at after they have taken time to consider their total relationship, its past, its present, and its future."

A SUMMARY OF THE FACTS

- Sixteen appears to be the critical age for sexual initiation. After this age, the percentage of adolescents who have sexual intercourse doubles.
- Fifty percent of teenage girls aged 15–19 have had sexual intercourse (up from 30 percent in 1971 and 43 percent in 1976).
- The greatest increase in teenage sexual intercourse is among girls. The rate among boys has been mostly stable the last few decades: 80 percent of boys aged 15–19 currently report that they have had intercourse.
- Teenagers are starting to have intercourse at younger ages. Currently, 17 percent of 14-year-old girls have had intercourse, compared to 10 percent in 1980. For 14-year-old boys, 21 percent had intercourse in 1980 compared to 32 percent in a recent study.
- Three out of five teenage girls who have had sex have had only one partner.

• Teenage girls 15–19 years old tend to have their first intercourse with a partner nearly three years older than themselves.
• About 25 percent of teenage boys who have had intercourse say that they planned their first time, but only 17 percent of teenage girls said they had.
• The increase in the proportion of females who have had sex before marriage has often been cited as evidence of the decline of the double standard. But research on the *feelings* one has toward the first partner indicates that little has changed over the last decade: Males are far more likely to feel a casual relationship with their first partner, while females are much more likely to be "in love" and/or have marriage plans. When asked, in one study, to describe their feelings after first intercourse, boys twice as frequently reported feelings of maturity, joy, and thrill; girls were nearly four times as likely to say they were afraid or worried, and twelve times more likely to say they felt guilty. The most glaring discrepancy was that only 1 percent of the males as compared with 25 percent of the females said they were sorry afterward. Another study found that 60 percent of teenage boys said they were "glad" after first intercourse; 61 percent of the girls were "ambivalent."
• "Sexually active" is a poor way to define teens who report having had sexual intercourse. Fully 38 percent of girls who were "sexually active" in one survey had not had intercourse at all during the month of the survey and 30 percent had had intercourse once or twice. Another study found that 15 percent of "sexually active" boys and girls had not had intercourse in the preceding three months. Yet another researcher reports that "sexual activity appears to be sporadic."

• Physician and researcher Louis L. Fine concludes from his observations and client experiences with teens that "the sexual act of a young adolescent is not, in most instances, one of erotic or physical pleasure. Nonsexual motivations—be they to gain peer approval, to escape from home, to rebel against parents, to express hostility, to search (vainly) for love, to compensate for depression, or to signal for help—are the most frequent underlying reasons for sexual behavior. At times, sex may be part of a close emotional relationship; such 'healthier' reasons, however, are definitely few and far between. For the most part, the sexual act of a young adolescent is hostile, angry, and self-destructive; it is not a demonstration of caring, sharing, or feeling."

• According to Robert Kolodny and colleagues, authors of *How to Survive Your Adolescent's Adolescence*, 33 percent of sexually experienced teenagers are so "frightened, disappointed, or guilty they can best be described as 'unhappy virgins.' "

CHAPTER SIX

RELATIONSHIPS AND SUCH

MOST TEENS are very quick to let me know that they really don't "date" anymore; they "hang out" or "go out." So, in the manner of an anthropologist, I probe further, asking them to enlighten me about how twosome relationships are now formed, and what terms describe what. Aside from some minor differences from region to region and school to school, the system and the definitions are mostly the same:

Going around: Liking someone and meeting them at school or at school-sponsored events. Or being with them at a party. Mostly you spend a lot of time on the telephone. Usually "going around" is what you do in junior high or mid-school.

Hanging out: Same as above. In some situations this defines a group of boys and girls getting together, not in matched pairs, just as a "group" doing something (or nothing) together, more or less. In other situations, the agenda is slightly more structured, at least to the extent that the number of males and females are even, more or less.

Going steady: When a couple is going with only each other over a period of time (this could be two weeks, or months). But it is mostly a term used by high school freshmen and sophomores, and in the Midwest and the South. The couple has to declare to their friends they are "steadies" and exchange some kind of token (ring, bracelet, chain necklace, or pin), which is returned when they break up.

Together: Same as "going steady" but a more "in" expression. Preferred by high school juniors and seniors, especially in urban areas. Some teens say "being together" or "going together." However, the best form is to let the word flow over the tongue, as in "we'retogether."

Being a couple: Same as "together" but the couple is "always seen together holding hands or kissing." Seems they are a "public" item.

Being promised: This is a more formalized "together." The guy gives the girl a ring, which she wears on the left-hand ring finger; star sapphires are very popular. The ring signifies that they are very serious about each other and maybe will get engaged when they graduate from high school. Some teens say it is a "pre-engagement," but that the couple wouldn't necessarily get married right after high school. In some schools girls who have a "promise" ring gain a certain status; in others they don't. Overall, teens tell me it is a custom mostly for kids who don't plan to go out of the community to college.

THE ARRANGEMENT

Whatever teens call these arrangements, they aren't as "loose" or "casual" as they appear on the surface. Getting together with a person of the opposite sex is carefully orchestrated, because it has all the potential of a one-way ticket to making an ass of oneself. Despite a teen's anxiety about the possibility of screwing up, trying to develop a relationship occupies much of their time and energy.

All teens say their initial or early-on venture into a relationship with the opposite sex is scripted just like a "date." If you string all of the parts together, you can conclude that, although "dating" isn't as formal and deadly ritualistic as it once was, it is still marked by rules mimicking the likes of "Happy Days." So I'll stick with the term "dating" because it describes the dynamics involved in going somewhere with someone of the opposite sex by prior agreement. Also, I've noticed that, all disclaimers to the contrary, teens use the word "date," and list concerns about "dating" when asked what they most want to talk about.

WHEN, OH WHEN?

At what age "should" teens begin to date? There really isn't any pat answer. Dating, like any other acquired social skill, needs to be approached so that your son or daughter is gradually allowed increasing independence and responsibility. I think that dating needs to be handled as a progression from adult-supervised group activities (parties, picnics) to unchaperoned group activities (which may include couples) to one-on-one experiences.

Now comes the great dilemma. When is a teen ready to go from one step to the other? There are two ways to look at it: calendar age and maturity level. The latter is more important than the former. But it's hard to peg a teen's maturity because some at 15 are as mature as the average 18-year-old. So most parents, for lack of a better measure, go by the calendar. Although it varies from region to region, and from family to family, there is general agreement among the parents I've talked to that teenagers under 14 should date in an adult-supervised activity, and those over 17 need not be chaperoned. In most communities, twosome dating is par for the course at 16. In some it is age 15 and even younger, especially for girls.

For years there have been attempts to muster support for parents of teens to band together and set uniform dating rules for their community. Presumably uniform standards would offer parents some measure of defense against the classic teenage argument, "But everyone else is!" It might work, but it will never happen. Probably just as well.

Setting up a set of rules within the family helps to keep the lines of communication open, and better conveys that the relationship between a parent and teen isn't one that is determined by a peer group—be that other adults or teens.

YOUR RULES

No matter what YOU decide about dating protocol, be sure to have a family round-table discussion in the formulation process. Teens who feel they are included in the process of rule making are much better rule followers. Otherwise, any attempt on your part to establish firm contracts with your teen will be a golden opportunity for youthful rebellion and manipulation. Hear your teen out. They encounter a baffling spectrum of standards and conduct—from the trampled-upon "nerds" to the "cowboys," "preppies," hyperactive studs, punks, and rockers—and need a little space to explore the vast territory. Don't set the rules in stone; leave a little room for adaptations, revisions, creativity. You may even have to acknowledge that some of your notions about dating are, well, like yesterday's meat loaf.

CURFEW, AND OTHER DATING GAME ISSUES

The mall. The great gathering place. The issue isn't shopping. It's over the amount of time teens want to hang out there. And what about curfew, dating on school nights, going to out-of-town concerts, camping out at the beach, and . . . need I go on?

All of these issues are not "issues" per se; they only become issues because teens generally want more freedom than we think they can handle. We don't want to be the last fuddy-duddy in America, but we don't want to see them crash from flying out of the nest too soon. And teens know how to make us sweat over every decision we are called upon to make—whether they can or can't do whatever it is we don't feel too at ease about. Teens pierce the heart of parental guilt when they argue that curfew, etc., is proof "you don't trust me." Trying to "be fair," most parents hopscotch down an ill-defined path, wondering if they are being "too strict" or "too lenient."

Unfortunately, there isn't any national survey of parental dating rules to provide you with an overview of what other parents are doing (as a way for you to know if you're in the ballpark). There are, however, some opinions about adolescent dating from a group of 400 psychiatrists surveyed in *Medical Aspects of Human Sexuality*. Granted, we don't know how many of these physicians were parents, much less parents of teens, but for what it is worth here is a summary of their answers.

1. *Should parents always know exactly where the adolescent is going on a date?*

Two-thirds of the psychiatrists said yes. Besides it being desirable for teenagers to let parents know what their plans are, they need to feel assured that they can call on their parents to help in any emergency without fear of recriminations.

2. *Should definite curfews be set for adolescents?*

About four-fifths of the respondents recommended the setting of curfews for all dates because having a limit promotes structure and responsibility. Without the curfew, parents have no way of knowing whether a delayed return is caused by an unexpectedly enjoyable evening or a real problem. Obviously, parents should progressively advance the curfew as the adolescent gets older, and as their son or daughter demonstrates the ability to handle responsibility.

3. *Should parents of adolescent girls insist on meeting all the boys they date?*

Nearly three-fourths said yes, because the boy who meets his date's parents is apt to be better motivated to act responsibly than one who can assume the date is private and insular. And, by meeting the boy, it is hoped that the factor of accountability will minimize some potential hazards. The boy almost invariably supplies the car and does the driving (which can leave the girl at the boy's mercy with regard to arriving at and returning from their destination). Another is the tendency for teenage boys to drink heavily, which can leave the girl in the plight of ending a date with a boy far less compatible than the one she started out with. The respondents noted parents need to be careful that the pre-date meeting not be interpreted as punitive or a form of chastity watching. I'll go a step further and suggest you make it a harmonious occasion to strengthen your daughter's pride in her home and family. And it's a good way to convey your approval of her having a social life.

4. *Should adolescents be allowed to date on school nights?*

A large majority said that dates on school nights should be restricted to special occasions; a small minority were equally divided between those favoring unrestricted dating and those opposed to any school-night socializing. Reasons for restrictions: homework and study take a lot of time; need for adequate sleep, since teens need a lot of sleep; and even the most sociable or infatuated teenager should spend some evenings in the company of parents and siblings or a sense of family will deteriorate.

STAGE 1

When setting up guidelines for dating, consider first the stages of adolescence and how each stage is a progression toward the capability to handle a relationship.

In early adolescence, contact with the opposite sex takes place when two or more members of one group arrange to meet with a similar-size group of the other sex. At this stage there is a lot of talk within same-sex groups about who likes or who wants to date whom, but little gets formalized.

When a party or gathering of some kind or another—the movies, meeting at the local shopping mall or swimming pool—is planned, it is preceded by whispers and note passing. When it actually occurs, there is much giggling, mild insults, and some shoving and grabbing. Since there is safety in numbers, if things don't go well it's the "group's" fault and no one is singled out as a failure.

Think of this stage as the "huddle" period. At dances or parties girls congregate on one side of the room, boys on the other, except for a few brave souls who are dancing in a corner. Only the coolest of the cool can be seen locked together in the middle of the floor.

BOY CRAZY?

In early adolescence girls are usually more interested in having dates than boys are. And they can be very persistent. Mothers of young teenage boys constantly complain to me about the girls' aggressive pursuit of their sons via the phone or notes passed at school. Says the mother of a 13-year-old boy: "We get an annoying number of phone calls where the caller, a girl, giggles, and then hangs up. He tells me girls are always calling and asking him to be their boyfriend, or to meet them for a kiss. He's shown me notes that are, well, sort of shocking. The girls ask him to have sex with them, say they love him, and so forth."

These mothers also observe that their sons seem bewildered by the lavish attention (not to mention the sexual invitations) bestowed upon them. And parents (and teachers) say that a vast majority of young boys actually demonstrate scorn or contempt for "girls." It's curious this "boy craziness" girls have in this stage of growing up, contrasted to the lack of interest or disdain boys show toward girls. Or is it?

Think about it. It should come as no surprise to us that, after some twelve years of cultural conditioning saying that boys are superior to girls, a girl gains in peer value and self-esteem when she is able to attract and have boyfriends. No wonder they are in such hot pursuit of boys; it is a form of trophy hunting.

Andrea Boroff Eagan, in her book for teenage girls *Why Am I So Miserable if These Are the Best Years of My Life?*, puts it this way: "Getting a date or a boyfriend sometimes becomes so important to a girl that she loses her whole sense of proportion about it. It's not hard to understand why this happens. Everything seems to give you the idea that getting a boyfriend is the most important thing you can do; that getting a boyfriend will make you happy, solve all of your problems, improve your disposition, clear up your acne. . . . No one comes right out and says those things, but they're implied."

Others don't agree that it is just social conditioning that makes girls so much more eager for boyfriends than boys are for girlfriends. A number of people in the field of adolescent sexuality believe the keen interest girls show in boys before it is mutual is more linked to the fact that girls "enter" adolescence approximately two years earlier than do boys. They are simply tuned into dating and relationships before boys are.

Some people feel, no matter what they attribute the difference to, that girls should be allowed to date at an earlier age. I don't think, in most instances, it's a good idea. While in a few cases there is some merit to this point, on the whole it's not that workable. Girls tend to date or want to date boys a year or more older, which means they could be involved in more than they can handle sexually. Older teenage boys definitely have a stronger sexual preoccupation (that's sex, not romance)—whether it be biological or sociological—than do girls in early adolescence.

STAGES 2 AND 3

One of the sure signs that Stage 1 has ended and Stage 2 has begun is when a teen's interest in a person of the opposite sex gets more selective. Middle adolescents form "couples" that last a lot longer than they did just the year before, although, for the most part, their contact between dates or meetings is still often the intimacy given at a distance via the telephone.

I don't have to tell you that almost all teenagers spend seemingly inordinate amounts of time on the telephone. It drives most parents up the wall. But being attached to the phone may be part of growing up, a security blanket. They can chatter away without either party having to deal with relating face-to-face. On the telephone, the teen can practice intimacy without the risk of looking foolish or being publicly brushed off.

Middle and late adolescence is when "dating" makes

more sense in terms of having developed the ability to make better judgments about one's own interests and other people's personalities. However, these stages are not very distinct. The time it takes your daughter or son to advance from middle to late adolescence depends a lot upon their individual development. Still, don't dismiss the fact that they may be rushed into dating one person more seriously than they really want.

As most teens arrive at Stage 3, late adolescence, they are under increasing pressure to have only one partner. For some it is internal pressure. They are ready to invest time and energy in maintaining an intimate relationship. Others are under external pressure to be a part of a couple, even if they don't feel so inclined, because dating around is frowned upon.

I've asked vast numbers of teens whether or not it was considered all right (at their high school) to date more than one person at a time. The majority say no. You can "go out with" (i.e., date) one person, not repeat the date, and start all over with another person, but after you begin to "go out" with one person a few times, "You can't date anyone else." The notion of playing the field has gone the way of the Nash Rambler. By the time a teen is a senior in high school, much of the campus (in many schools) looks like Noah's Ark; males and females walk around in pairs.

SETTING LIMITS

As you design rules governing your teen's dating, you need to bear in mind that a teen's cognitive development does not always closely parallel physical maturity. The capacity for abstract thinking, judgment, and conscience evolves slowly, and this process is often far from complete in the early to middle years of adolescence.

No matter what age level is used to determine dating eligibility, or what other criteria you use, you need to set some limits for early adolescents. All in all, when it comes to dating in the form of being alone with a partner, I think it is wise for parents to put their young teen in the slow lane.

David Mace, a family and marriage counselor, agrees. He says that dating too early intensifies social tyranny, and sexual and financial exploitation. A summary of his views: (1) You either have a date, or you can't go to the party. If you don't find a partner, then you are a failure. This leads to insecurity and shyness in boys and girls. (2) Dating too early fosters a subtle form of mutual exploitation. Our cultural mores encourage the boy to go as far as he can sexually with his date. If he doesn't, he is a failure. If she allows him to, she is a failure. (3) Girls tend to exploit boys financially. They expect expensive dates and expensive gifts. Boys under 16 normally earn very little money but are often required to spend large sums on a date. Girls also exploit their parents. They demand expensive dresses and often want a new one for each big occasion (see Herbert Miles's *The Dating Game*).

Admittedly, Mace was deliberately trying to paint a glum picture. Still, he's not too far off in his assessment of the exploitation inherent in the young teenage dating scenario. But it isn't so easy to convince young teens that they would be better off waiting a while before hopping on the date merry-go-round. There is tremendous pressure on young teens to date and on parents to let them. The battle cry is, "Everyone else gets to!" Even if dating brings on more anxiety than pleasure, the race is on.

Sanford Dornbursch, a Reed-Hodgson professor of human biology, sexuality and sociology at Stanford University, in his study of dating patterns, found: "Here is a case where social processes ride roughshod over biological processes. I was shocked that social norms effectively wiped out the influence of individual sexual development." He also says: "The impact of social expectations regarding the appropriate age for dating is powerful, and . . . the influence of biological development of the individual is, for this set of behaviors, relatively unimportant. The peer group, usually fairly homogeneous in age, exerts pressure on its members to engage in dating behavior that is typical of the age group at that time. Youths could be rejected for deviating from the dating patterns of their peers" (see *Sexuality Today*'s article).

In short, as a parent you are under the gun. My advice is to hang tough. Try to set 15 as a minimum age for what I label couple dating, or, as some teens describe it, "car dates" (when a couple goes off by themselves in a car). As most states don't allow teens to get a driver's license until age 16, you will have better luck holding off "car dates" with your son than your daughter. You may have to relent once in a while and allow your under-16 teen to go out with another couple in a car, depending on your ability to withstand the onslaught of pleading or to sidestep the issue. Again, don't make your rule a negative one; talk to them about the positive side of waiting—"just a little."

I'm not suggesting that young teens should not have the opportunity to try out their repartee with the opposite sex. Make them feel welcome to have informal "hanging-out" gatherings in your home and encourage them to be part of recreational get-togethers. Actually, this goes for all ages of teens. The more you are understanding of their need to form relationships, the less likely they are to be secretive or leap into involvements that are detrimental to them. You might get some flak from your young teen, but most accept the "rules" if they seem fair.

WHAT TEENS WANT IN A DATE

Before the "couple" stage sets in and the question is moot, teens think a lot about what they like and don't like in a "date." In *Co-Ed Magazine*'s survey about dating preferences, a vast majority of the guys said they liked girls to look "foxy." The girls said they liked guys to look "natural" (a slight majority), or "macho" (a close second). And the guys said they liked girls who are their age and about their height, while the girls voted for guys who are taller and a little older.

In addition to those attributes, there is one more that never seems to pop up in surveys. Yet, when you listen to teens, you can hear it plainly: The person must be acceptable to their friends. If he or she isn't, they won't go out with them, at least not for long. Gaining status through dating the "right kind" of person, or losing status by dating the "wrong kind" of person, is a great consideration. Hear what Greg, age 16, has to say about this aspect of the dating game: "When everyone likes the girl you are going with, your friends are, well, a little envious. That makes you feel really great. You don't want other guys to make a big play for her, but she has to be someone other guys would like to have. I wouldn't date a girl who doesn't fit in because then I would be out of everything."

Other teens back up Greg's assessment; many have told me of being dropped by their friends when they dated someone who failed to meet their crowd's approval. It makes them feel like a traitor to the person they like, but the pressure to conform takes precedence.

All of this means that you will meet great resistance when you try to play matchmaker or try to patch things up. When you think Person X seems like a great kid and your teen is lukewarm, the reason may have less to do with that person's sterling qualities than with how they fit into your teen's group. It may seem ridiculous to you that your teen would allow peers to influence such a personal choice, but to them it's serious business. Teens say they hate it when parents push someone on them, and they feel foolish trying to explain why they don't want to date someone their parents think is terrific. Just remember, their reasons make sense to them and, in the end, they go out on the date, not you.

DATING RITUALS

While the specifics of dating hinge upon the norms of the particular group your son or daughter identifies with, there are some common denominators. For example, there was wide agreement among a group of 100 teenagers polled as to their thoughts about dating. Not that I think this group speaks universally for teenagers—I don't (it was a small sample, the readers of *Co-Ed Magazine*). Nevertheless, I think you'll find their responses an interesting addition to your understanding of teen life today. "Hanging out" with the gang was what most guys and girls said defined "dating" among themselves and their friends. The next most popular activity, "going steady," nearly tied for second. And as for who pays: More girls than guys (50 percent to 29 percent) thought the cost should be split, with two-thirds of guys and one-third of girls saying the guy should pay. About three-fourths of the teens said they only dated once in a while, with 24 percent claiming to date a lot. As for the "perfect date": A dance or a party rated higher than having a burger and seeing a movie. Going to a school game or watching TV didn't generate much enthusiasm.

The response about who asked whom for a date had a perplexing twist. When the girls were asked if they had ever asked a guy for a date, 86 percent said no. But wait a minute, something doesn't add up. When the guys were asked if they had ever been asked out by a girl, about half said yes and half said no. Maybe girls didn't think they took the first step. Or maybe they didn't want to admit they took the initiative.

THE ETERNAL QUESTION

We've already discussed sex in the teenage years; now we have to consider where sex is most likely to occur. And the answer is on a date (or going around, etc.).

You are wise to be concerned about how your teen, especially in early adolescence, might handle the sexual pressures that can arise on a date. A young teen's judgment about the sexual expectations of their "date" isn't usually very good. For example, look at what psychologist Aaron Hass discovered when he surveyed teens about sexual expectations on a first or second date: To the question, "What do you usually hope will happen sexually on a first or second date?" the majority of boys responded that their main concern on a first or second date was to get to know the girl better and expected to kiss or neck. When he asked boys, "What do you think most girls hope will happen sexually on a first or second date?" their most common response was "I wish I knew," or "I have no idea." When he asked girls, "What do you usually hope will happen sexually on a first or second date?" most said they were primarily concerned with getting to know the other person better and expected only kissing. Some girls added that if they really liked the boy probably a little light petting might happen. To the question, "What do you think most boys hope will happen sexually on a first or second date?" approximately one-third of the girls thought boys wanted to pet, while the others thought that boys were primarily interested in getting to know the girl.

Yet, for all of the "just wanting to know the other person

better" and expecting only to "kiss or pet," teens often end up having sex on a date, ready or not. However, Hass found a difference in males and females: Fewer boys than girls replied that they had sexual contact on a date even though they did not really feel like it. He notes that this difference may reflect the greater social permission given to boys, and therefore less inner conflict, about having sex. He explains that it is likely many boys are trying to act out a myth about their gender: "Males should always be ready, willing, and able to have sex. The need to be 'a man' may override any sexual discomfort or lack of genuine desire." Furthermore, Hass goes on to say: "Because of sex-role expectations, girls are less likely to assume an aggressive posture. Therefore, the possibility of a sexual encounter is more likely to arise when the *boy* feels like having relations." Fifty-seven percent of the boys reported having sexual contact when they didn't feel like it—with little difference between younger and older. Still, that adds up to slightly more than half!

Hass uncovered a striking difference between the younger and older girls. There was a significantly greater number of younger girls, ages 15–16 (65 percent), compared to older girls, ages 17–18 (48 percent), who reported having sexual contact on a date when they didn't feel like it. Hass concludes that there may be three possibilities: "Perhaps the older girls are more likely to give themselves sexual permission and, therefore, would simply want sex more. It is also possible older girls are feeling less conflicted and more sure of their sexual values. And finally, the older girls may be more confident in relating to boys and, therefore, be able to be more assertive about what they do or do not want."

What Hass's research and other similar studies clearly tell us is that *both* males and females have great difficulty in dealing with the sexual byplays inherent in being alone with another person on a date. Judgment gets better with age; the younger the teenager, especially girls, the more likely it is that they will buckle under to sexual pressure.

HAVE A GOOD TIME!

Dating is a way of knowing someone better, spending time with a person you like, and a way to socialize. But it's more than just a social event for virtually all teens, especially those beyond early adolescence. The desire to pair up and be alone together *is* connected to feelings of being sexually attracted to the other person, and can be tagged, for lack of anything else more descriptive, sexual "urges." It really shouldn't surprise as many parents as it does that sex play and exploration are commonplace on a date.

However, I've found that the sexual side of dating tends to be ignored by most parents, who either have the capacity for a remarkable degree of self-deception or, consciously or unconsciously, have blocked out what happened on their high school dates. It comes back in spades when their teen gets interested in someone. Take, for instance, the feelings one parent told me he had when it suddenly occurred to him that his daughter would be alone with a guy who might be expecting something more from her than a peck on the cheek. He says, "I didn't really think much about my daughter's excitement about going out with 'a really terrific guy' until I opened up the front door and there he was, 'the date.' I was suddenly overwhelmed with the urge to slam the door in his face. All I could envision was my young stud days and the endless wrestling in the backseat." When I pointed out to him that his daughter might want more than a peck on the cheek from this particular "terrific" guy, he just slowly shook his head back and forth. I know how he feels; it is very difficult to imagine our daughter or son *enjoying* more than a friendly kiss.

It's one of our hardest tests: letting them go out that door knowing full well that it is perfectly natural for them to be attracted to the person they're dating, and that there is bound to be something sexual (not necessarily sex, but "something") going on before they return to safe harbor.

Even though you worry about premature sexual involvement, you can't refuse to allow your late adolescent son or daughter to date until they are certifiably "mature," tempting though it may be. You have to rely on the hope that you have given them enough self-confidence and information about sexuality to make good decisions, and that they will be able to handle whatever situation comes up. More than likely, dating for them will be a good experience: They might even have that good time we always tell them to have.

ENDLESS LOVE

I'm often asked if a high school steady relationship, one that has gone on for several years, won't lead to marriage either in the waning days of school or right after graduation. A parent can't help but be worried. None of us wants to see our son or daughter getting married that young. The probability of your teen seriously planning to get married, or actually getting married, is slight: Only about 8 percent of girls ages 15–19 and 2 percent of the guys in this age group are married. But that's enough to at least alert us that we can't be complacent and totally dismiss the possibility of our son or daughter becoming a statistic at the marriage bureau.

As the old sports cliché goes, "The best defense is a good offense." Your best defense, if they appear to be moving toward marriage, is knowing some of the reasons why teens marry, and then becoming informed about prevention.

Fortunately, getting married as a teen isn't the "in" thing

to do. They won't get much support from their peers. Most teens don't think it is a good idea to be married until they are over 20; they peg the time between 20 and 24 as "the best age to be married." And teens see marriage as a serious commitment. They don't plan on the trauma and heartbreak of divorce; 90 percent say that when they get married they expect it to last the rest of their lives.

Why do some teenagers marry? There are any number of reasons—wanting to get away from home, being madly in love—but a sizable majority (approximately 30–50 percent) of teenage marriages occur because of pregnancy. Many teens who get married have a very limited sense of their future, of the grand array of opportunities ahead for them in the adult world. Or their sense of self-esteem and self-confidence is severely dented. They are incredibly insecure about their own ability to form other relationships or to be loved by anyone but the person who now vows to love them forever. For those teens who lack the ability to see beyond their current problems or limitations, marriage may be viewed as a ready solution. For some it is, but for most it isn't.

Although the numbers are few, there are teens who marry because they want to have sex but feel it is immoral to have sex before marriage. Ruth, a woman in her early twenties, explained to me why she married at 17: "I was so guilty about how close my boyfriend and I were getting to having sex. We did everything but. We were so afraid we would lose control, and after years of being told it was 'better to marry than to burn,' we eloped." (For the record, Ruth got divorced at age 19.)

The greatest deterrent to a teen getting married comes from within themselves: their plans to enjoy life as an adult, to travel, to explore, and to be a happy and successful person. But the teenage years can be a time of such uncertainty that some teens lose their balance; they become too emotionally handicapped to understand the consequences of their actions, or so dazzled by their feeling of love for another person that they can't see beyond it. Usually this is only "temporary insanity," and they recover.

INTERFERENCE STRATEGIES

If your son or daughter seems hell-bent on getting married, or moving in with their lover, you'll have to step in, and quickly. I'm convinced parents have to help their son or daughter avoid such an obvious mistake. Don't rely on the hope that "this too shall pass"—they may be in way over their heads.

Use as much tact and influence as you can muster to get them to postpone their plans. You may have to acquiesce to their living together, but try to do everything you can to make them reconsider. Living together, while not bound by legal entanglements, has almost all the shortcomings of marriage for a teenager. As getting married is substantially worse for a teen than living together, I'll mostly concentrate on how you can help them defer marriage. But, basically, the strategies are the same for either situation and you can substitute the words "living together" for "marriage" in most instances.

Use a carrot, not a stick. When a parent becomes angry and sets out to oppose at any cost their teenager's avowed intent to get married, it only serves to spur the teen on. A determined teenager can go off to another state, seek permission to bypass your legal consent (if that is needed), or simply run off and get married when they reach the legal age. Your tactic is to buy time, and time is on your side.

Don't start out by listing all of the negatives. For some young teen couples, marriage works out. Admit that your son or daughter may be one of the lucky couples. Anyway, a teenager has a very hard time with "other-people" generalizations as examples; they see themselves as being immune to the pitfalls. Listing all of the reasons why they shouldn't get married only leads to a big debate, and one that parents could too easily lose.

Tell your son or daughter they may be able to overcome the obstacles and make a go of it. Be clear that it is not "marriage" in itself you are concerned about, that you believe in the rewards of being married to someone you love. All you are asking is that they make a reasonable effort to take a clear look at their own situation and relationship before they leap. Recommend a marriage counselor, or that they attend a prenuptial class. Point out that a teen needs to be prepared, because teenage marriage is risky, with about 60 percent of these marriages ending in separation or divorce within five years. Marriages that take place when a person is a teen are two to four times more likely to break up than are marriages of people in their twenties.

Convey to your teen that they are much more likely to have a marriage that is successful if they wait just a few years or even just one more year.

Remind your son or daughter that, while marriage may bring some pluses into their lives, they need to consider the minuses. Get them to sit down and make a list of not only what they would gain, but what they would have to give up. Steer their thinking about marriage as based solely on loving each other to a vision of a relationship between two individual people, each with their own tastes and personalities. Compromises and respecting the other person's ideas about music, movies, household chores, life, money, friends, sex, and time are not only important, but essential.

DESPERATE MEASURES

As a last resort, you can try bribery. It may not work, but —if the situation is getting desperate—nothing ventured, nothing gained. A good friend of mine, I'll call him Ray, was distraught over his 18-year-old daughter's proclamation around the middle of April that she planned to get married "the day after graduation in June." She was a B+ student, was accepted to a good state college, had a lot of friends, and was, as he summed it up, "a normal kid until the last six months when she can't think of anything but HIM." Ray tried every way he knew to reach her on a commonsense level—discussions, and showing her articles and books on the problems inherent in getting married too young. All was to no avail. She turned a deaf ear. The man she wanted to marry was 24, and she feared "he wouldn't wait," or that they would "drift apart." Ray discussed his last-ditch plan with me. He would promise her (and her fiancé, Josh) that *if* they postponed their wedding date until she was 20 he would give them the down payment on a townhouse, or, if they rented an apartment, he would pay half of the year's lease. And he wouldn't insist on her going to college. She could work, live at home, bank her salary, build up a nest egg, and they could spend holidays and weekends together at Josh's place.

Frankly, I thought it was a plan doomed to fail. To my amazement, it worked. His daughter and fiancé had lengthy discussions over the next two weeks and decided to accept his offer. After working for six months, she decided to go to college and postpone getting married "for a while." This all happened four years ago, and I couldn't resist pulling aside his daughter, who is still single, at a party not long ago to ask her how she felt about the situation then, and now. She laughed and told me, "My dad was such a sly old fox. I didn't feel pressured because he kept saying, 'It's your decision.' Josh got married last year, and I hope he is very happy. I've chalked the whole thing up to a very narrow escape."

Since Ray's experiment, I've discovered that friendly persuasion in the form of bribery is more effective, and more common, than I had thought. Many parents under the pressure of a declaration of their teen's intention to wed have told me they offered to pay for a trip across country (with a best friend, not the intended), a horse, help with applying to the Peace Corps or a student exchange program—whatever they could manage to come up with—to entice their son or daughter to wait. In almost all cases, once the teen had some time to think about it and an incentive to wait, they decided not to get married.

WHAT TEENS COULD USE MORE OF

Wherever I travel to talk to teens, it is very obvious that the most neglected form of teenage relationship is friendship between the males and females. And it's so ironic. Teens who have good friends of the opposite gender are much less likely to exploit each other and are a lot less vulnerable to the tyranny of dating because they are not dependent upon a "date" for a sense of self-worth and identity. Friendship can uniquely provide the kind of mutual support and affection that transcend a relationship based on being "lovers."

So, make it easy for your son or daughter to have friends of the opposite sex. I know that sounds very simple, but it isn't. You may not be aware of how difficult it is for your teen to have a friend who isn't a potential, or bona fide, boyfriend or girlfriend. Listen to the following tales.

Amy, age 16: "I've known my best friend, Pete, since we were both 4 years old. We have a lot of fun together and share the same interests. It never used to matter, but now the kids at school and our parents won't let us alone. My dad thinks I'm a little too old to hang around with Pete. The kids tease us about being 'steadies.' Nobody understands that we just LIKE each other. My mom never lets up on me. She's always saying, 'Pete's such a nice guy, when are you going to see the light and grab him?' And Pete's mom has been acting funny lately. Last night when I went over to his house to do some homework and listen to his new record she opened the door with 'No wonder Peter doesn't have a real girlfriend; everyone thinks you have your brand on him.' Are we weird just because we don't feel, well, you know, for each other, but still love each other?"

Jeff, age 15: "I really get along great with a girl named Kathy. We used to live next door to each other and go fishing and sleep over in our backyards. I have a lot of friends, mostly the guys on my soccer team. But Kathy means a lot to me. She never puts me down, and we have a lot of laughs. Now I'm in the ninth grade and Kathy's in the tenth. We still live real near each other and we like to hang out together, but it's getting impossible. My mom says Kathy is too old for me and tells me that I should date someone my own age. Her mom says I'm too young and it doesn't look right for her to spend so much time with me. Christ, we don't want to get married! We just want things to be the way they used to be. Do you think a boy and a girl can be just friends? Why is everybody on our case?"

Why indeed? Once a person becomes a teenager, every aspect of our society tries to discourage guys and girls from being friends: Society assumes that any transaction between the genders (past puberty) has to be linked to sex for guys and romance (which could lead to sex) for girls. Strangely, at the same time society puts great store in the virtue of boys having "girlfriends," and girls having "boyfriends." And the message that something is "wrong" if they aren't paired up starts when they are very young. How many times did you hear your son or daughter asked, when they were a toddler (smirk on the questioner's face): "Do you have a boyfriend/girlfriend?" And if your kid looked bewildered and said, "I'm too young for that stuff" (a logical response), the adult wasn't the least embarrassed to have asked such a dumb question!

Our society doesn't put much stock in the idea that males and females can be friends, or that they really want to be. Boys and girls are taught that they have little in common, or that they are natural enemies, that is, The Battle of the Sexes. This notion of male and females as adversaries placed on the battlefield of love and sex, each trying to manipulate and capture the other, paves the way for girls and guys to think of each other only as dates, mates, or foes.

Consider the ultimate effect of sexism and separatism on how we deal with each other. It is difficult for men and women to be friends. We hesitate to spend too much time together if we aren't lovers; it could give others the wrong impression. Yet friendship can break down the barrier of sex-role stereotyping and open new frontiers of dealing with each other as equals. Unlike love, which can be fickle or unrequited, or sex, which can be pressured, friendship is founded on personal choice.

HAVING FRIENDS

Do all you can to support your teen's friendly impulses and encourage them to have friends of all kinds: same sex, opposite sex, introverts, extroverts, music fans, computer wizards, backpack enthusiasts, bookworms, etc.

Respect your teen's preferences. Maybe they only want one "best friend." Fine. Without pushing them, suggest they not reject the possibility of being friends with people on various levels. Not everyone likes to do exactly the same thing at the same time, and not everyone shares the same tastes in music, sports, or anything else. Emphasize the point that friendship doesn't have to be exclusive. It can be fun to do something with one friend that another friend doesn't enjoy.

Try to get your teen to understand that friendship doesn't mean you are exactly like each other, but that you care for each other. You love a friend because they are who they are and they reciprocate.

To help your teen develop the knack of having friends and of viewing male and female friendships as both desirable and natural, you can do the following:

- Be sure to include a mix of single and married people in your own social gatherings, and make it clear that it doesn't matter if the numbers are even or if males and females aren't matched up.
- Encourage them to have friends over, or help them organize a group to go somewhere. Don't make a boy-and-girl list of names, just list "friends."
- Assume friendship, not romantic interest, when your son or daughter mentions "liking" someone of the opposite sex, and let your teen know that is your assumption.
- Talk about the friends you had in school and those you have now, why you chose each other as friends, and how you nourish these relationships.
- Discourage your son or daughter from dropping a friend when a "boyfriend" or "girlfriend" appears in the picture.
- Reduce sexist teasing or exclusion by not tolerating it. When you hear your son or daughter say something like "Girls (or boys) are stupid," let them know that it's a stupid generalization.
- Try to get them to reconsider their plans to exclude someone because "we have to have the same number of boys and girls."

• Be creative about language. Talk about pals, buddies, friends. Try to avoid the terms "girl" friend (a friend that is a girl) and "girlfriend" (you know what that means). Describe relationships as gender neutral. For example, "Jim's friend, Kathy," or "Jim and Kathy are good pals."

Putting a premium on friendship and guiding your teen to be free-flowing and gender blind when it comes to having friends mean you'll need to give them some extra doses of love and understanding. Shore them up when they are showing signs of buckling under the pressures of conforming to the rules of the traditional boy/girl game to placate their classmates or other unenlightened people.

A SUMMARY OF THE FACTS

• Over the past several decades the age at which teenagers begin to date has declined, so that the median age for the start of dating is approximately 13.
• At any given age after 12 more girls than boys are dating.
• Teenagers who begin dating at an early age will probably date more frequently during their entire adolescence.
• By age 14 to 15 roughly half of all adolescents have dated. Almost all adolescents have dated at least once by the time they are 18–19 years old.
• Most adolescents, especially girls, move gradually toward advanced levels of sexual intimacies, such as petting and intercourse, through a series of dating and going-steady experiences. Because of cultural changes and more opportunities for privacy, today's teenagers are likely to move more quickly into physical intimacies than they did before 1965.

• Almost three-fourths of the teenagers surveyed in Jeanne Warren Lindsay's study said it is all right for couples to live together before they marry. About 29 percent felt living together was "wrong." Other teens in this study only approved of living together if the couple was planning to get married (27 percent of the girls, 25 percent of the guys). It is interesting to note that more Born-Again Christians than Catholics disapproved of cohabitation, while the views of the Protestant teenagers fell between the two groups.

• According to a study at Washington's Urban Institute, if a girl between the ages of 14 and 17 gets married, she is over two and a half times more likely to break up with her husband than if she weds between the ages of 20 and 24. If she marries at 18 or 19, she's at a 60 percent higher risk than if she waits until she is in her early twenties. Statistically, at least, sons fare better than daughters. If a teenage guy marries between 14 and 17, he's twice as likely to divorce than if he marries between 22 and 24. Between the ages of 18 and 21, it's somewhat better, but not by much; the chance of divorce or separation is still 50 percent higher than if he waits until he is past 21.

CHAPTER SEVEN

SURVIVING A BROKEN HEART

NEIL SEDAKA HAD IT RIGHT in his song "Breaking Up Is Hard to Do." It's a wretched experience for the one who wants to break up and for the one who doesn't. Falling in and out of love is hardly a unique experience, but to each person struck by the sick-at-heart emotions of a relationship gone sour, it feels very unique. More so to a teen. Everything in the teen's perspective is intensely personal, immediate. They rarely think about the possibility of love not being "happily ever after." When they begin to feel wobbly about being in love with the other person, or become interested in someone else, they anguish over how and when to break up. If they are the one who gets the bad news, they are grief-laden, heartbroken. And because teen romance, especially among young teens, is so fickle, having a heavy heart is a chronic ailment.

BEING THERE

When your teen is desolate, forlorn, and miserable over someone breaking up with them, you want to console them, soften the blow a little. But what to do? Parents are in a tight spot. Cheerfully attempt to nudge them into thinking it's not the end of the world and I can guarantee you'll hear the familiar teenage lament, "You don't understand!" Pour on the sympathy and bring on the chicken soup and they may wallow in a woebegone state, making everyone in the family miserable. Still, I get so many questions and comments from teens about breaking up that I can assure you they need your help, even when they don't act like it. Sometimes, in their confusion, they put up a shield of solitude that's difficult to penetrate. Or, because they are feeling rejected, there is a tendency to be touchy, or lash out. It's safer to take their anger and unhappiness out on the people closest to them, their family, than on their ex-lover or friends. Remember, when in the throes of melancholy, none of us can muster up much logic, be hale fellows well met, or have any enthusiasm for making glowing plans for the future.

Each situation has its own story, so my advice is to simply be there for moral support, and listen to their tale of grief. Then, take the next step: Share with them some strategies for "getting over it."

STRATEGIES FOR SURVIVAL

First of all, acknowledge that picking up the pieces takes real effort. Convey that you *do* understand. After a breakup, tell them they can expect to feel bad for days, weeks, or even months before they realize how much they've learned about themselves and relationships. Psychologists agree that a person can expect to go through five basic stages of mourning: denial (when you can't believe it's over), anger, depression, bargaining (when you think you can do something to get back together), and, finally, acceptance. Sometimes, these emotions come all at once. Your teen needs to know that going through these stages is normal. Emotions of suffering and grieving are part of getting over a relationship that meant something. It's not crazy, or immature; it's very human. And here are some things you can suggest they do to dull the hurt:

- Allow the sadness and pain to come, but don't dwell on it. Accept it, but don't conjure it up.
- Don't blame yourself for "mistakes," or feel you were inadequate. Don't tear yourself apart with "if onlys."
- Eat right and exercise because your emotions will heal quicker if your body is in good health.
- Go ahead and cry as much as you want; it is a cleansing relief. But try to perk up when around your friends; they may tire of being around someone in mourning. Save crying for when you are alone.
- Maintain a schedule and don't get behind in schoolwork, because it helps to keep your outer world in order when your inner world is in chaos.
- Play tennis, racketball, Ping-Pong—let your anger out (pretend the ball is you-know-who). Then, channel your anger into doing something physical (jog, swim) or something creative (write a poem, play the piano, make a special gift for a close friend).
- Don't play the breaking-up scene over and over in your mind, trying to assign blame. Think about what was right, and take pleasure in that.
- Put your thoughts on paper. It's a good way of getting a perspective, of settling things. Write when you want to; quit when it feels finished.

These strategies aren't a panacea for mending a broken heart, but tell your teen that, because they have helped other people, they are worth a try. Then, because teens have a penchant for romantic drama, calmly discuss that remaining distraught over an expired relationship isn't necessary to prove how much a person "really loved" the other. Accepting the fact that the relationship is over doesn't demean what you felt, or make it less than it was. In other words, they don't have to feel duty bound to prolong the pain to affirm they cared a lot.

WHEN THEY WANT IT TO BE OVER

Surprisingly, little attention is given to the emotions and the pain of the person who wants to break up a relationship. Teens, who lack experience in the love game, are especially baffled about how to end (or be less involved in) a relationship. You can give them some things to think about to help them clarify their thoughts, and some guidance on how to approach the situation.

Discuss why ending a love relationship means the erosion of dreams and hopes you shared with someone special. "Hope dies hard, even when you know the reality of your experience was completely different from your dream," observes counselor Ahn Williamson. However, hedging about telling the other person the relationship is no longer satisfying isn't fruitful. Delaying can gnaw away at you. For example, Williamson adds: "Staying in a relationship, for the sake of appearances, or because you don't know how to end it, breeds resentment. And resentment makes you old and ugly before your time." Why do so many people put off the inevitable? Again, according to Williamson: "Some people put off breaking up a relationship because they fear being alone, or they don't want to feel guilty."

One of the problems teens have in telling the other person they want to break up is being sure it is indeed "over."

I asked a group of teens for a list of clues that indicate a relationship is on the wane. Pass it on to your teen (they are more apt to pay attention since it is from the mouths of "peers").

- One or both of you start looking for excuses to pick a fight.
- He spends more time working on his car, and less time with you.
- She or he never wants to be alone with you anymore.
- You start telling little white lies to each other ("I have to study for history," or "My folks say I have to stay home all day today").
- When he or she says something that bugs you, you don't try to straighten it out, you just say "forget it."
- You put each other down in front of friends.
- You feel like a hypocrite saying anything about the future.
- You find yourself comparing him or her to another person you think is outrageous (parent, that means neat or terrific).
- You wish they would understand that you need more space.

Once your teen has come to the conclusion that they want to tell the other person they need to separate, totally or somewhat (but not one minute sooner), you can help them map out how to go about it. Ask them to be, above all, very gentle and tactful. It takes guts to face another person who is very likely to be angry and hurt by what they will have to say. So, Rule 1: Explain it in person; it is a whole lot kinder than writing or phoning. Rule 2: Be firm. Don't waffle; it's easier to make a clean break than to shatter the relationship piece by piece. Rule 3: Be fair. It's rubbing it in to bring up the other person's shortcomings. Don't try to skirt around the point, or try to pick a fight to salve the conscience. Better to tell the other person they really enjoyed the good times they had, they hope to continue being friends, that no one is to blame, but it's time for them to branch out, make a change.

THE FINAL SCENE

No matter how gently one treats another person or how certain one is they want to end a relationship, your teen needs to know there is no painless way to break up. But tell them that being honest about your feelings is far better than hurting the person even more by reluctantly and resentfully staying with them. Remaining on friendly terms may not be possible because, even though things have been very tense between two people, and even if they themselves have thought about splitting, the rejected person will suffer a bout of heartbreak. Being jilted is a tough experience. Rejection turns what were once loving feelings into emotions of hurt and anger. It takes a while for the heart, and ego, to mend.

NOT SETTING PATTERNS

If you are comfortable about it, share with your daughter or son your own experiences with love gone awry. Don't compare your lost love(s) with their situation. Simply talk about what you learned about yourself and the intricacies of developing a relationship. Resist being flowery or generalizing; be personal and specific. For instance, when my first real steady asked for his ring back, I was devastated. How could he do that? We were the perfect couple; everyone said so. When I finally dried my tears—weeks later—I thought back about our dates and conversations. I had to admit I usually planned our dates to suit myself. And the conversations had been one-way: me on broadcast. In my enthusiasm of going with the guy with the most beautiful black hair and blue eyes on my high school campus, I failed to notice that he was very shy. I insisted we go to every party on the calendar and invited as many people as could fit into the car to ride along with us. The more the merrier —but not for him. He silently suffered, except for a few feeble efforts to plead that "we be alone" and "go to a movie." In storybook fashion, we were the quintessential "opposites attract" couple; in fact, we had little in common. I learned you can't make someone be what they are not, and you can't change some deeply embedded traits of your own. I also vowed that, next time, I would pay attention to what a person is like under their good looks, and make a real effort to hear what someone I care for is saying.

What is important here is that you let them know that, although it doesn't seem so likely at the time, you do gain something from a loss. Ask them, when they are emotionally far enough removed from the trauma, to objectively reflect upon the interactions between the two of them. Can they stand back and analyze what they would do differently next time? For example, they can think over whether they or the other person was too needy or too demanding. Was the relationship based on mutual interests and caring, or the fear of not having someone? Did they change in their feelings toward the other person? Did the other person seem different after they got to really know them? Stress to your teen not to sell themselves short; everyone is not suited to everyone, and with a little time and experience they will find someone who suits them better. They can take a long look at what they really want and what they are able to give in a future relationship. And knowing yourself is the best way to know how to relate to someone else.

Ahn Williamson suggests parents encourage their teen

to understand the essence of their experience to avoid making the same mistakes again. The reason this "self-examination" is widely recommended by counselors is that these early love experiences, if not given some contemplation and closure, can set patterns that are repeated endlessly in adult life. If a person's self-confidence isn't reestablished, and if they don't comprehend the "me" contribution to the "we" of a couple, they may go from one unsatisfying relationship to another.

Finally, stress to your teen not to rush into another romance. Sometimes people fall "madly in love" on the rebound to fill a grinding emptiness or to patch up a shaky self-esteem. But if one isn't really over the loss of a breakup, the next relationship doesn't ever jell. Tell them they will be more prepared for another relationship in the future if they give their heart a cooling-off period. And—most important—with a little patience and time, love will return again. Tell them also not to let being hurt in one relationship prevent them from giving their heart away again.

A SUMMARY OF THE FACTS

There are no research data (or at least I couldn't locate any) about teens' surviving a broken heart. All I can tell you is to rely on experience and instinct. I did find two studies of interest on college-age people:

- Women fall in love more frequently than men, but men fall in love more quickly.
- Men hang on longer to a dying affair than women, and women end more romances than men.

CHAPTER EIGHT

HOMOSEXUALITY/ HOMOPHOBIA

DON'T ASSUME THAT YOUR SON OR DAUGHTER is not interested in the subject of homosexuality simply because it hasn't been brought up. Teens *are* curious. They want to know what homosexuality is, how you can tell if someone is homosexual, and what "causes" it. Despite their curiosity, they usually hesitate to ask questions. Even if you haven't said anything negative, or given them the impression it is "the worst thing ever," most teens believe it is terrible, to be avoided at all cost. Homophobia—fear and hostility toward homosexuality—is rampant among adolescents. Thus, they may feel the topic is so full of worms it's strictly off limits for a family discussion.

The traditional scriptural prohibitions condemning homosexuality so permeate this culture that even members of enlightened denominations are influenced by those negative messages to varying degrees. It's not so surprising then that many people can be tolerant of homosexuality in principle, but feel uncomfortable about it closer to home.

However, there is an important difference between having personal feelings of discomfort about homosexuality and actually discriminating against homosexuals. I'm in agreement with psychologist Sol Gordon and counselor Judith Gordon: "Regarding rights and discrimination, we stand with the majority of well-informed people in the country who believe that people who happen to be homosexual are entitled to the same civil rights as heterosexuals. We strongly feel that any other position is simply bigotry."

Some teens are afraid that if they show an interest they will arouse suspicions about their own sexual proclivities, especially if they aren't really involved with a particular person of the opposite sex, if they are having homosexual dreams or fantasies, or if they have a crush on someone of the same sex. They can believe they are perverted, weird, and disgusting.

A more critical reason to bring up the subject is the possibility that your son or daughter is beginning to be aware, or feel certain, that their sexual preference is for partners of the same sex. If you show openness and understanding about homosexuality, they are more apt to confide in you.

Even if homosexuality isn't a personal issue for your teenagers, it's important for them to be informed because they have classmates, friends, relatives, or acquaintances who are gay or lesbian—some openly, some secretly. Being aware equips young people to handle not only the fears and hostility they may have experienced, but the homophobia of others. And that's no small thing. As Letty Cottin Pogrebin points out: "While homophobia cannot prevent homosexuality, its power to destroy female assertiveness and male sensitivity is boundless." Conformity is celebrated among teens and even minor eccentricities bring on ostracism or taunting. When your son or daughter displays the slightest deviation from stereotypical "masculine" or "feminine" fashions or behavior, they are fair game to be called queer, fairy, faggot, dyke. They may have been, or are now, suffering from sarcasm or, worse, harassment. They can be very upset by this, but too embarrassed to go to you for help.

Hence, take the initiative. Use a book, a magazine article, or a TV news item to get a discussion going. Be as factual as you can, and stay calm if they spill out some very homophobic comments or use the occasion to tell offensive jokes. Remember that they are parroting the anti-gay sentiments of most of their school chums, not to mention the party line of some churches.

SEXUAL ORIENTATION

The best way for your teen to understand what homosexuality is, or isn't, is to hold discussions in the context of sexual orientation: the preference for sexual partners of the same sex (homosexual), of the opposite sex (heterosexual), or of either sex (bisexual). First of all, although theories abound, no one knows what causes homosexuality. There is a lot of evidence, however, that homosexuality is not a choice; it is a deeply felt, compelling orientation.

Most psychiatrists and researchers agree that heterosexual and homosexual orientation are not distinct entities, but rather points on a continuum. Usually, sooner or later, one sexual orientation dominates. But how or why this happens is not clear. Ironically, for all of the recent proliferation of studies about homosexuality, the best information about sexual preference is still derived from the classic studies by Alfred Kinsey and his colleagues in the late 1940s and early 1950s. To better understand sexual orientation they devised a scale of possible sexual behaviors:

0: Exclusively heterosexual behavior
1: Largely heterosexual but incidental homosexual behavior
2: Largely heterosexual but more than incidental homosexual behavior
3: Equal amounts of heterosexual and homosexual behavior
4: Largely homosexual but more than incidental heterosexual behavior
5: Largely homosexual behavior but incidental heterosexual behavior
6: Exclusively homosexual behavior

The Kinsey study estimated that about 10 percent of white American males could be ranked exclusively homosexual between the ages of 16 and 55; 4 percent on a lifelong basis. During adolescence or young adulthood, 37 percent of the white male population had at least one homosexual experience that lead to orgasm. As for females, Kinsey suggested that, by age 40, 19 percent had had an erotic experience with other women, but only about 2 to 3 percent were mostly or exclusively homosexual for all of their lives. (Although Kinsey's work is well regarded, keep in mind these statistics were compiled a long time ago.)

You *can* tell your teen that having a preference for partners of the same sex isn't abnormal: It is similar to being left-handed in a world of mostly right-handed people.

One of the most interesting things, I think, Kinsey brought to light is that the stringent dichotomy of "heterosexuality" and "homosexuality" is a false one. It's much more likely for people capable of both kinds of responses to shift in varying degrees at different times in their lives. Kinsey noted: "The world is not divided into sheep or goats. . . . Nature rarely deals with discrete categories. Only the human mind invents categories and tries to force facts into separated pigeon-holes. The living world is a continuum in each and every one of its aspects. The sooner we learn this concerning human behavior the sooner we shall reach a sound understanding of the realities of sex." Although Kinsey makes a lot of sense, for the purpose of discussion, given our society's limitation on language, I'm stuck with using the terms "homosexual" and "heterosexual."

Teens also wonder about "bisexuality," aka "AC/DC" or "switch-hitting": persons who have sex with either male or female partners. There isn't much factual data about it. However, sex researchers Masters, Johnson, and Kolodny, in their book *Human Sexuality*, say: "Bisexuality is a form of sexual experimentation or a deliberately chosen sexual style. Relatively little research has been done on this subject, but it appears to be a comfortable option for some people while being unthinkable to many others."

SAME-SEX EXPERIENCES

A very essential point to bring up with your teen is this: Sexual experiences with someone of the same sex do not necessarily mean a person has a permanent homosexual orientation. During their childhood or adolescence most adults had some sexual experiences with persons of the same sex: playing doctor, fondling, mutual masturbation, and so forth and so on. That kind of sexual experimentation doesn't mean much in the area of predicting the future. As health writers Howard and Martha Lewis observe: "Adolescents do a great deal of exploring of their new sensations, often propelled by a drive for physical release. For many youngsters bursting with sexual impulses, sex is sex."

Convey to your teen that being attracted to someone of the same sex and getting involved in sexual play is a perfectly natural aspect of growing up. It's not unusual at all.

Be very reassuring because many teens can be confused by their same-sex experiences. Although young people generally enjoy same-sex contacts and remain relatively free from shame and embarrassment in early adolescence, they can become anxious and guilt-ridden when they enter mid-adolescence. Boys, because of the widespread fear of male homosexuality, are more likely than girls to feel disturbed over their same-sex experiences or their sexual interest in a friend of the same sex. Eminent sex educator Lester Kirkendall, in a survey on sexual worries and concerns, found that about one out of five boys said they were, or had been, concerned about homosexuality. In a group of college-age males, the proportion is even higher. Sadly, when some boys feel *any* special closeness to other boys they become tormented by thoughts of being gay.

Girls are less panic-stricken over their same-sex experiences because two girls can hug, hold hands, and be together all of the time and no one makes a big deal of it. In fact, demonstrativeness among girls is considered "feminine." And it is more acceptable for a girl to go through the stage of having a deep crush on another girl. Even if sex play takes place, neither girl involved is likely to see herself as lesbian. Typically, as girls' relationships with boys increase, their crushes on other girls decrease. Still, your daughter might be worried that her feelings or her experiences aren't quite all right.

At any rate, your son's crushes on someone of the same sex are as normal as those of your daughter. What is worth noting is that your teen's anxiety and confusion can be greatly reduced or eliminated if they can talk about their feelings and yearnings with you. Look at it this way: Teenage crushes are really all to the good—a healthy movement away from childhood self-centeredness toward the maturity of thinking of other people in a caring way.

SELF-DISCOVERY

How do people decide that they are mostly or exclusively homosexual? There isn't any one pattern. Some people say that it was a slow process; only after a time of being sexually confused about their orientation did they begin actually to think of themselves as gay or lesbian. Others say they suspected their same-sex orientation even before they had actual sexual experiences with someone of the same sex, because they never felt comfortable or satisfied with opposite-sex partners. For some, discovering their sexual identity came after a long struggle to fit into the heterosexual mold and finding out it wasn't for them. For many people the awareness that they are primarily attracted to and sexually compatible with others of the same sex doesn't come until they are way into adulthood, maybe not until they have been married and have children; for others it is crystal clear in elementary school.

However, it is usually in the teen years that gay men and lesbian women first become aware that they aren't sexually attracted to people of the opposite sex. And that alone makes them different from most of the crowd. They know they are different but feel they are alone with their secret. In the teenage world social pressures to be "normal" are so intense that most teens keep their feelings hidden from family and friends. They are often terrified that their parents or friends will find out before they feel ready to tell them, and even more terrified to make any overtures to someone to whom they are attracted. Wayne Pawlowski, a clinical social worker who counsels gay youths, says: "Kids dealing with gay feelings go through adolescence in a skewed way. Heterosexual teenagers learn how to date and establish relationships. Gay kids don't learn any of that. What they learn is to hide their feelings" (see "Growing up Gay," *Newsweek*). Because of the external pressures to be a "regular" guy and girl and their internal confusion, many, if not most, homosexual teens become alienated and lonely; they have a great deal of trouble establishing any kind of ordinary friendships.

"Girls are generally more isolated than boys," says Joyce Hunter, a lesbian activist and social worker. "They have fewer resources for meeting other young lesbians than young gay men have for meeting each other." Author Rita Mae Brown agrees and notes, "Gay women are an invisible segment of American society."

All of this means that you'll have to make every effort to be alert if your son or daughter is sending signals your way. Don't conjure up something that isn't there, but don't look the other way either. Many parents don't have to deal with their child's homosexuality because they prefer not to know, or prefer to deny it. Try not to fall into that trap.

OUT IN THE OPEN

Here is some food for thought. No matter how or when people become aware of their sexual preferences, most gay men and lesbian women say the hardest thing isn't coming to terms with themselves, it is telling their parents. And with good reason. Most parents feel as though they were hit with a ton of bricks when they hear their child say, "I'm gay." Being unsettled, ambivalent, appalled, and any shadings of emotions in between are very parental reactions. Emotions often follow a pattern. Initially it's a shock. Next grief follows: a mourning for lost dreams of weddings and grandchildren. Then many parents are overcome with shame and guilt. "Where did I go wrong?" is a nearly universal question.

Of course, all of us hope that if the situation arose we would suppress any misgivings and react with immediate loving acceptance. All good intentions aside, it's easy to see why even the most liberal, the most tolerant parents find themselves caught up in a churning of heavy-hearted emotions. Let's face up to a sobering moment of truth: It's one thing to be nonjudgmental and accepting of homosexuality for others, but quite another to deal with it as a parent.

As parents, we aspire for our offspring to be happy and hope they will enter the ranks of adulthood with as little going against them as possible. Although homosexuality doesn't provoke the hostility or discrimination it once did, none of us is naive enough to dismiss the reality that a lingering and often hostile prejudice still exists. It's perfectly normal to worry about what others, especially those close to you, "will think." Friends and family may be very accepting, but chances are their reactions, at first, might range from outright horror to subtle rejection. We are only too well aware that being homosexual, even in today's world, isn't easy. It's simply not what we had in mind for *our* kids.

Added to a parent's concern over the possibility of social isolation or insult is a new, more deadly element: AIDS, the epidemic striking so many gays. It is terrifying to think your child could be in danger of contracting this fatal disease.

By making the point that many parents are jarred and upset at learning their child is gay, I don't mean to imply that every family goes into a tailspin. Not at all. Some parents are very supportive and accepting from the moment their child declares these feelings. And there are families who, after an initial shaken reaction, develop a new sense of solidarity from the opportunity to express how much they value each other, unconditionally.

All I'm saying is this: Should one of your children someday tell you they are homosexual, you need to be prepared for how you will feel and how you might react.

If your child makes such an announcement, make every effort not to panic. Don't say anything you can never take back. Rejection only serves to sever family ties, and you may never mend the wounds inflicted by your inability to talk things out calmly.

It is so difficult for young people to talk to their parents about their feelings about homosexuality; don't make it any harder. They aren't doing anything "to you" (as in, "How could you do this to me?"); they are doing what is right FOR THEMSELVES. Counselor Elizabeth Canfield, who works with gay and lesbian children and their parents, says, "Intimate, caring relationships are hard to come by, but do exist in same-sex couples. I think parents need to get to the place where they care more about the *quality* of their kids' relationships than the *plumbing* of the partners with whom their kids tie knots. The significant point is the 'wow factor,' that sense of total well-being one experiences when everything fits: mental, physical, emotional, spiritual. This factor is not present for people who have to grit their teeth and fantasize about someone of the same sex while being expected to be attracted to someone of the opposite sex."

It helps to consider how much courage it takes for a gay son or lesbian daughter to tell their family. They are showing a great deal of trust by confiding in you and signaling their need for your acceptance. All in all, it's better for them (and for you) that they bring the subject out in the open rather than worrying about being "found out" and living a life about which you are kept in the dark or from which you are excluded. "The secret life is more dangerous and damaging than most of us realize," says Canfield. "The twisted, absurd way of growing up when there's so much to hide. The lying, cheating, and deceiving often continue into adulthood, and marriages can be contracted based on ever more lying and sneaking to bars after hours. And on and on."

So be clear you appreciate being told their feelings; you hope communication between you will always be open.

WHAT TO DO

Don't waste energy trying to figure out what went wrong. The simple fact is nothing did. Of all the influences about which a parent can feel guilty, this is one over which we have no control. Dominant mothers or unemotional or absent fathers don't make sons into gay men or daughters into lesbians. What counts is the here and now.

Try to keep things in perspective. Homosexuality only describes sexual orientation, it doesn't describe the total person. It's a sex style, not a life-style. Most gay men and lesbian women manage their lives as well or better than their heterosexual counterparts. Studies are in agreement that, aside from choosing partners of the same sex, gay men and lesbian women, on the average, are no different from heterosexual men and women in gender identity, self-esteem, relationships with parents, and satisfaction with their lives. Keep this in mind: Homosexuality is neither uncommon, harmful, or a mental illness.

The specter of AIDS may be the most alarming aspect for you. While it is small comfort, in the shadow of AIDS, psychiatrists, counselors, and gay organizations are emphasizing "safe sex." Information on protection against AIDS is being widely disseminated. There is a lot of evidence that the fear of AIDS has led to a new sense of responsibility among young gays.

GOING SLOW

Now there is a fine line to walk. While you are being supportive of your teen's sexual feelings, you need to encourage them not to rush into making a firm commitment to homosexuality. This doesn't mean discounting their sexual preference as a "passing phase." Acknowledge that they may be totally correct about their sexual orientation and it may be unchanging. Nevertheless, going slow makes sense. Teens go through so many changes on the road to adulthood that they may find themselves feeling differently later on about exclusive preference, or any desire at all, for partners of the same sex.

Urge them not to jump to conclusions and to keep their options open. Make it clear that most experts on the subject feel that deciding during early adolescence that one is definitely and permanently homosexual may be premature. It's also true that by late adolescence most people are clear about their sexual affinity. However, there are significant numbers of young people whose sexual orientation, be that homosexual or heterosexual, isn't defined until later in life. As Sol Gordon and Judith Gordon put it: "A homosexual is a person who, in his or her adult life, has and prefers sexual relations with members of the same sex."

I suggest you ask your teen to consider seeing a counselor—to help sort out feelings and enhance a positive sense of self-esteem, not to have homosexuality "cured." Not only does "conversion" or a "cure" not work, it can backfire. Therapist Judd Marmor compares the difficulty of changing a person's sexual orientation to that of converting left-handedness to right-handedness. "Attempts to make 'righties' out of 'lefties' can result in severe emotional problems, stuttering, or learning disabilities." So choose a counselor with care; it has to be someone who understands sexual orientation.

Even though your teen's sexual preference is very clear to them and they feel they are well adjusted and are able to deal with life all right, a counselor can provide some guidance on conducting a safe sex life. I think it would be a rare adolescent who wouldn't have some problems in dealing with the realization that they are (or could be) homosexual in a heterosexual world.

If your teen is reluctant about seeking counseling, don't force it. After all, same-sex orientation in itself isn't a reason to seek therapy. But given the reality that gay and lesbian youths are very vulnerable to their peers' hostility toward homosexuality, counseling can provide welcome relief.

COMING OUT

I also recommend you urge your teen not to rush into publicly "coming out" by joining a gay organization. Although a case can be made for the positive aspects of doing so (it is important for people to join together to overcome discrimination against homosexuality, and to promote an individual and group pride and identification), there are some practical considerations. For a teenager, the positive factors—support, information, and a way to make friends—may be overshadowed by some negative consequences. On the one hand, as I've pointed out, his or her commitment to homosexuality can be premature. On the other, discrimination could limit their future choices. While gay civil rights have improved greatly, the legal advances have a long way to go toward eradicating inequities against persons who are homosexuals: Society is still mostly "antigay." Discrimination may not be as overt or as harsh as it used to be, but it can play a subtle role in terms of admission to some professional careers and graduate schools. Unless things have changed just recently, known homosexuals have been banned from being employed by the FBI, the CIA, the military, and law enforcement services.

Talk to your teen about the findings of Grace and Fred

Hechinger, who did a study of homosexuals on college campuses. They found that "virtually all the counselors they met, homosexual as well as heterosexual, urged homosexuals not to declare themselves at this young age." Dr. Thomas Merrifield, a psychologist at Berkeley's counseling services, is gay and yet said, "I wouldn't urge anyone to take a personal risk" because he sees "a continuing cruel conflict between the relatively protective college environment and the outside world, particularly in the professions."

Aside from the repercussions of the prejudices of strangers in society, your teen needs to assess how publicly "coming out," beyond family and a select group of other people, will affect them in their personal life, particularly at school. Outright rejection probably won't happen among their close friends, but outside of that circle it is likely. Also, teens who are tolerant of homosexuality on an intellectual level may not want to hang out with someone who is gay. They might manage an awkward friendship, but typically the relationship cools off. Then there is the fear of AIDS, which could be a factor in a teen's being ostracized at school. Says one gay student who belongs to a gay group outside of his high school campus, "The kids at school wouldn't speak to me if they knew. They think if you touch someone, or eat lunch with someone who is gay, you'll get AIDS."

If your teen, despite your urgings to postpone making a public declaration, does go ahead, there is a bright side. More sources of counseling and services for gay youth are now available. *Newsweek* magazine, in a terrific article, "Growing Up Gay," found that support groups have been formed in many cities. In northern Massachusetts, for example, members of Gay and Lesbian Liberated Youth of the North Shore meet weekly. Says a social worker with the group, "Peer support limits the isolation these kids feel."

There are many resources now available for parents as well. The National Gay Task Force (80 Fifth Avenue, New York, NY 10011) can put you in touch with other parents of gay children. Another support organization, which has parent groups throughout the country, is FLAG (Parents and Friends of Lesbians and Gays, Box 24565, Los Angeles, CA 90024). Also, check the resource list in the back of this book for books and pamphlets.

IN THE BEST INTEREST OF ALL

The most constructive thing you can do is to be supportive, no matter what your children feel they need to do. All a negative or rejecting attitude does is put an unbridgeable gap between you and your child. However you feel about your child's declaration of homosexuality, focus on loving them, and being there for them. Letty Cottin Pogrebin gives some of the best advice ever: "Don't worry how to raise a heterosexual child; worry about how not to be a homophobic parent."

A SUMMARY OF THE FACTS

- In 1974 the American Psychiatric Association declared that homosexuality "by itself does not necessarily constitute a psychiatric disorder." In effect, the association removed homosexuality from psychiatry's list of "mental disorders."
- Most of the research on self-discovery of homosexuality suggests that this process is most likely to occur during adolescence for males and at a somewhat later time for females. Although some lesbians come to a firm discovery of their sexual preference in adolescence, a large number do not adopt homosexuality until after a heterosexual marriage.

• Alfred Kinsey found that, by age 19, more than 35 percent of boys have reached orgasm through masturbation, or via oral or anal intercourse with another male. Among teenage girls, Kinsey found that between 6 and 11 percent actively engaged in sex play with another female. Kinsey's figures for girls are much lower than for boys, probably because only behavior leading to orgasm was counted. Among girls, same-sex activity—kissing, fondling, or masturbating—may be frequent but rarely leads to orgasm.

• Research by Masters and Johnson found that the physiological sexual responses of homosexual men and women are no different from those of their heterosexual counterparts.

• Bell and Weinberg's study found that homosexual men and women lead stable lives and, on the average, are no different from heterosexuals in gender identity and self-esteem, and some are considerably happier and better adjusted than heterosexuals as a whole. The researchers also noted that gay men are more likely than lesbians to have difficulty accepting their homosexuality, which they commented might be because homosexuality is more often seen by males "as a failure to achieve 'masculine' sexual adjustment," whereas lesbians "more often experience their homosexuality as a freely chosen rejection of heterosexual relationships."

• Masters, Johnson, and Kolodny state that there is no evidence that homosexual teachers seduce or molest students more frequently than do heterosexual teachers. If anything, they note, "it looks as if the opposite is true."

• A recent review of the research evaluating the performance of homosexuals and heterosexuals on a variety of psychological tests concluded that psychological tests can't distinguish between homosexuals and heterosexuals and that there isn't any evidence of higher rates of emotional instability or psychiatric illness among homosexuals than among heterosexuals. Concluded researcher Evelyn Hooker, "Homosexuality as a clinical entity does not exist. Its forms are as varied as those of heterosexuality."

CHAPTER NINE

HMMM, WHAT ABOUT CONTRACEPTION?

YOU MAY BE UNEASY broaching the topic of contraception because you don't want to give your teen the impression that you are condoning them having sex or, in some way, encouraging it. Relax. There is no evidence that if young people know how to prevent pregnancy they will be indiscriminate about sex. In fact, studies show that teens don't rush into sex because they know about contraception. Some teens do postpone sex because they are afraid a pregnancy will result, but they are a small minority. There is, however, a lot of evidence that, where sex is concerned, young people are most liable to get hurt by what they *don't* know. Anyway, it doesn't make any sense for young people not to be fully knowledgeable about how contraception works, because knowing how to control fertility is fundamental to being in control of one's own life.

THE ESSENTIAL FACTS

Make it crystal clear that pregnancy doesn't "just happen" —a twist of fate—it's exactly what's supposed to happen when people have sex and don't use a method of contraception to prevent it. Pregnancy is the natural outcome of unprotected sexual intercourse; that is how the human species reproduces. Sounds so elemental, doesn't it? Yet it is one of those biological truths teens don't seem to easily comprehend because they have difficulty connecting future consequences to immediate behavior. Some teens understand "how babies are made" all right, but rely on wishful thinking that "it won't happen to them." Reveal to your teen that four out of five teenagers who have intercourse without contraception will eventually start a pregnancy. Many teens get pregnant *the first time* they have sex. The message to get across to them is this: *Trusting to luck is too big a gamble when the stakes are your own life.*

Even if your son or daughter disclaims any interest in hearing about how to prevent pregnancy, forge ahead. They may be trying to avoid having a conversation with you about contraception because they don't want you jumping to any conclusions about their potential or actual sex life. You may be surprised to know that many teens worry about showing an interest in the topic of contraception because it might give their parents the impression they are planning to have sex. Sadly, some teens say they would rather risk getting pregnant than having their parents find out they need to know about, and use, birth control, because then their parents would know they are sexually active. I know how illogical that sounds, but teens are not golden examples of rational thinking.

GETTING YOUR MESSAGE ACROSS

To pave the way for them to accept the responsibility of avoiding a pregnancy, you have to lay the groundwork by letting your son or daughter know how much you value having them avoid the trauma of such an event. Talking to them calmly about how concerned you are about an unintended pregnancy has a side benefit: You are saying how much you care about them and their well-being.

Don't talk around the topic. The possibility for misinterpretation is too great. My experience working with teens leaves no doubt in my mind that they need to know whether or not you disapprove of them having sex, and that you can accept them being sexually active far better than a pregnancy. Be *very* specific: "Never risk the disaster of an unwanted pregnancy. Having sex means always using contraception. No matter what. Sex is never an emergency." In the best way you can, press upon them the point that, regardless of how you feel about their sexual decisions, they need to consider *for themselves* their own personal capacity to take the responsibility for preventing pregnancy. If they don't feel they can use a method of contraception effectively, or if they are unsure about their ease in communicating about birth control with their partner, they will be at risk for pregnancy. Encourage them to postpone sex until they can be responsible for contraception as a positive step in their ability to think for themselves.

AGAINST THE GRAIN

Now I have a confession. I made it sound as if all you had to do was to lay your cards on the table and voilà! the problem would be solved. In actuality, you are going to meet some tough obstacles. I have to caution you that getting your teen to feel comfortable about having anything to do with contraception won't be easy. The whirling winds of society push them into the opposite direction.

Teens are squeamish about the subject because they know the vast majority of adults—teachers, politicians, preachers, neighbors, relatives, counselors, physicians, and last but certainly not least parents—don't approve of teenagers having sex. Contraception is the bold undeniable evidence that they are, or are planning to, which means they face disapproval at best, condemnation at worst. And there is little encouragement from their peers, who are as confused as they are. Don't count on sex education at school coming to the rescue. Contraception is treated with kid gloves. A lot of schools omit the subject from their "sexuality" classes, or brush it aside as "something for later" in favor of touting abstinence, or they promote "saying no" exercises (aimed at girls, all claims to the contrary).

Contraception, as a topic of conversation in our society, is either hushed up or tagged "distasteful," "not natural," "crude," or "immoral." And those attitudes make it very difficult for parents to break the sound barrier and get across to their teen the message that contraception is proper, acceptable, and an expected responsibility.

Chalk it up to the lingering prudishness of our society, which can't make up its mind whether it wants to prevent premarital sex or prevent teenage pregnancy by encouraging contraception. Movies, music, TV, commercials, magazines, and novels play sex to the hilt as romantic, exciting, titillating. But none of these dazzling sexual adventures informs teens that contraception is readily available, much less desirable. In sexually explicit films, and in steamy TV soaps, people fall in and out of bed, have affairs, abortions: only contraception is censored. Have you ever seen a scene on TV where a woman slithers away from a passionate embrace saying, "Don't go away. I'll be *right* back after I put in my diaphragm." Or a man whisper in his throbbing partner's ear, "Darling, before we go any farther I must put on my condom." Not likely.

The worst of it is that teens have less wherewithal than adults to see through the hypocrisy. Too many of them believe that birth control destroys the romance and spontaneity of sex because that is what they have been led to believe. And at the same time, the underlying theme is "Good Girls don't unless Swept Away by the passion of the moment." So even though you may be a lone voice in praising the use of contraception, keep repeating "never have sex without contraception" or your teen might succumb to the pervasive script portraying True Love unencumbered by the nitty-gritty of birth control. And that careless kind of love is a sure route to an unwanted pregnancy. Ask your daughter or son: "How romantic is it to worry about pregnancy, to take that kind of risk about your future?"

COULD IT BE YOUR SON OR DAUGHTER?

Worrying about the possibility of your teen becoming a statistic in the teenage pregnancy rates is valid. It's downright scary. The United States leads all other industrialized nations in the number of teenage pregnancies, and is the only nation where it is on the increase. (For the record: The U.S. rate is 96 per thousand, Netherlands is 14 per thousand, 35 in Sweden, and 45 in England and Wales.) Researchers trying to figure out what makes the difference, given that teenage sexual activity is about the same in these countries, found one central point. Other countries focus less on preaching about the immorality of sex than ours and are more committed to their role in providing young people with contraceptives and realistic sex education to prevent pregnancy.

Obviously, our national ambivalence about sex and contraception is not going to fade away in this generation. You just have to do your best not to let it make your teen a hapless casualty. Although you might rather they not have sex, don't let your feelings allow you to detour from the goal here—helping them accept the responsibility for contraception when they make the choice to be sexually active.

TAKING RESPONSIBILITY

The picture isn't entirely glum. While most teens who are having sex still don't use a method of birth control all of the time, teenagers on the whole are getting more consistent about using contraception. And they are doing this in spite of all the obstacles put in their way. I think you'll gain some insight into how teens deal with all of this by reading what teenage patients wrote in a patient comment book at a family planning clinic. As one teenage girl penned: "I'm here on my first visit. I'm sort of nervous and very squeamish, but I've found that the people here have been *very* helpful. I mean, I can express my fears and hang-ups without any hesitation whatsoever. I really have a hang-up about becoming pregnant. But I feel more confident now. Still that darn pelvic examination . . . oooh! I was feeling tense and sort of sick to my stomach when I heard what I had to go through. But after seeing that short li'l movie, I feel much better. I realize that the exam won't be so gruesome and long after all. It really is a good idea!!!"

And another teenage girl put it this way: "My boyfriend and I stopped in today to prepare ourselves for our future. I see everyone watching everyone else nervously. All I can say is it is great that we care what happens to us and our society. But what hurts is that we are the ones rejected from society for going here and caring. This does not bother me though because I am 'ME' and always will be!" A particularly poignant remark was made by an almost-adult guy or girl while waiting in a clinic: "I'm still nervous about being here. . . . Is this Me? *Me* who spent 13 years in Catholic schools, with nuns and priests? If they could see me now they'd never believe it. I guess I'm growing up. I thought I'd never grow up, like Peter Pan and the Lost Boys. Sigh. Reality is a large cold splash of water in the face."

You have to give them, and the others like them, a lot of credit for having the gumption to take the steps necessary to avoid an unintended pregnancy.

TWO TO TANGO

Don't fall into the trap of emphasizing birth control as primarily the girl's responsibility because she is the one who ends up being pregnant. True enough. But the emphasis on the woman's role in reproduction is more a sign of the times than a biological fact. Up until the pill became widely used by women, men were taught they were "responsible" for "getting her pregnant." Condoms were the most popular method of birth control. Unfortunately, the expectation that men should use precautions has mostly faded from our collective memory. It would be better all around if we got back to the biological reality that "it takes two to make a baby," and teach both daughters and sons that contraception is a 50-50 responsibility.

Basically, this means getting across some simple information (don't overestimate their grasp of these basics either): To prevent pregnancy you have to keep the sperm from fertilizing the egg or prevent the fertilized egg from embedding itself in the uterine lining. Contraception is known by other labels—family planning, or birth control—but a lot of teens just say "the pill," so you need to mention those terms also when you initiate a discussion. And you'll have to address one of the great misconceptions a good number of teens (especially girls) have about contraception—that it is harmful. State that, on the contrary, pregnancy poses a greater risk to a teenager's life and health than the use of any method of birth control.

Stress the point that teens have special needs regarding contraception, and no one birth control method is right for everyone. Which method is the best depends on the teenager's individual physical maturity, their ability to use a method properly, how often they have intercourse, and their relationship to their partner.

Let's take a look at what methods seem to be effective and appropriate for teens and what hardly works for them at all.

EFFECTIVE METHODS*

NOT GOING ALL THE WAY

This doesn't mean "not doing it" or abstinence, but rather expressing sexual feelings without the kind of intercourse—having the penis in the vagina—that leads to conception. This is known, depending upon the slang of the day, as "heavy petting," "mutual masturbation," or "outercourse." (Obviously, the most effective pregnancy prevention method is abstinence.)

But you have to get across the point that a couple has to be *very* vigilant that the seminal fluid doesn't get near the

* For more detailed information see the resource list.

woman's vagina because sperm can swim upward and reach the uterus if any of the man's semen gets near enough to the vagina to enter it. And that can occur if the tip of the penis is only near the vaginal opening. I admit that this method may not be the best solution, but it beats taking a pregnancy risk.

Oral Contraceptives

Oral contraceptives (OC), in general, are safe for teenagers. Women under 18 are at less risk of serious adverse effects from OCs than are older women, especially those who do not smoke.

They are the most popular medical (prescription) birth control method because they are one of the most effective and convenient methods. In addition, they can be used in private and will protect the woman from pregnancy even when sex is unplanned and spontaneous. And that alone is a major advantage of using OCs for a teenage girl—it saves her the embarrassment of actually being seen using a method, and relieves her from having to make the decision to use something if her partner disapproves or might criticize her for being "too prepared."

There are *all* different kinds of oral contraceptives, and what a woman takes is not one pill but a series of them. Pills work by changing levels of hormones (estrogens and progestins) in the body to stop ovulation. Most pills are a combination of progestin and estrogen. There are some pills that contain only progestin. The combination pills are more than 99 percent effective in preventing pregnancy. The progestin-only pill is slightly less effective, about 97 percent.

Before prescribing OCs to a teenage girl, a clinician will balance the risk versus benefit to her based on her individual physical condition and medical history. Usually, OCs cannot be used until a young woman has established regular menstrual periods. Side effects, such as weight gain, nausea, and depression, with one type of OC can often be corrected by switching to another. Some clinicians recommend that while a woman is in her teens she use OCs and then change to another method of birth control when she is older. There is considerable agreement among clinicians that the medical risks from OCs for teenagers are fewer than the risks they face from pregnancy.

And there are some benefits from taking OCs: reduction in the incidence of various menstrual disorders, including excessive menstrual bleeding, irregular and painful menstruation, and premenstrual tension.

THE INTRAUTERINE DEVICE

It is difficult to predict accurately what the status of the IUD will be because in 1985 the major producers stopped manufacturing and marketing most of them. Basically, the IUD doesn't seem to be an alternative for anyone anymore.

For the record, this action has little effect on contraception options for teens because the IUD had few benefits for them. Most clinicians say they should have only been used by those teenagers who could not use any other method, and then only under close medical supervision. The data indicated that teenagers using the IUD who had not borne children were at a higher risk of developing infections. Another major concern was the rare but real potential for future infertility.

DIAPHRAGMS

The diaphragm is becoming increasingly popular among young women because it is safe: It has no serious side effects (sometimes there is an allergy to the latex or the spermicide). It is a rubber cap with a ring around the edge, which fits over the cervix. It must be fitted by a clinician and used with spermicidal jelly or cream. The diaphragm/jelly method is about 95 percent effective if used properly. But the range of pregnancy figures can be anywhere from two to twenty for every hundred women because women vary widely on just how well they use it.

This is really a good method for teens because it offers protection against sexually transmitted diseases and cervical cancer. The greatest drawbacks to its effectiveness are "human error." Some women try to "outguess" their ovaries, using the diaphragm only when they think they are ovulating. And teenage girls are the worst record keepers about their cycle. Besides that, the diaphragm for a teenage girl presents other problems: There is a lack of privacy necessary for consistent use; it is a symbol that they were prepared to have sex because it can be inserted several hours in advance (sex didn't just happen in a moment of passion); and they consider it messy. All of these minuses mean that a teenage girl is apt to take a risk "just this once" rather than use her diaphragm.

However, in one study of highly motivated teenagers, who were carefully instructed and given close medical follow-ups, the pregnancy rate was as low as 2 percent. So it's worth recommending. Especially for teenage girls for whom consistency is a part of her life and whose sexual relations don't take place on the spur of the moment.

The Condom (Rubber, Safety, Prophylactic)

The condom, used together with contraceptive foam, is 97 percent effective in preventing pregnancy, which is almost as good as OCs. Without foam it is about 80–85 percent effective. Condoms come in all types: lubricated, thin rubber, animal membranes (one size fits all, folklore to the contrary). Most of the failure rate is due to the fact that men don't know how to use them properly. And more than a few teenage guys say trying to get them on is so embarrassing they aren't worth the trouble.

A guy should know that the condom has to fit tightly over the penis leaving a reservoir of space at the tip to hold the semen. Some condoms are made with a reservoir, others are not. So he needs to make one if the condom is the type that doesn't. The condom should be rolled carefully onto the erect penis just before intercourse and carefully taken out of the vagina after ejaculation, with the guy holding on to it to make sure he doesn't spill any of the semen.

Advantages to teens: Even those of the best quality are relatively inexpensive, don't require a prescription, are readily available in supermarkets and drugstores, and can protect each partner from passing on a sexually transmitted disease—even genital herpes. That last advantage is really very important. Sexually transmitted diseases are at epidemic proportions. Many are damaging to the reproductive organs (especially of women) with few symptoms apparent to the person.

As effective and safe as the condom is, it should be a popular choice of birth control for teens. Unfortunately, not as much as you might think. As simple as the condom is as a method, it isn't so simple for a guy who wants to use it to do so. The problem goes back to Good Girl/Bad Girl teachings. As one teenage guy explains, "When you tell a girl you have a condom it is one big turnoff." Why? Because some girls view it as an action that proves he puts her in the "Bad Girl" category—a girl that is too easy about sex. In other words, the condom indicates to her that he knew she would have sex with him. So when a guy has a condom it can mean to some girls, as Jan, a 16-year-old, put it, that "he doesn't really care about you, that he isn't really serious about you; he thinks you're sleazy. He doesn't respect you."

One teenage male tried to help me understand just how difficult it was for a guy to "be responsible" by describing girls' reactions to a condom: "It's like showing a silver cross to a vampire—they cringe at the sight of it—and demand to go home immediately."

Of course, there are quite a few girls who say they are "grateful" when the guy has a condom because this relieves them of "being prepared" themselves. It may also mean—although they don't consciously recognize it—by ignoring the need for the condom, they can still hang on to the notion (for themselves, at least) that sex was spontaneous. Some girls told me they insist that the guy use a condom—they are not about to get pregnant. However, you can't count on your daughter, especially in early adolescence, being able to put aside all of the implications involved.

Some teenage guys complain that the condom takes away the feelings of pleasure (feels as if they are in a shower with a raincoat on is the usual comment). But I like what one teenage girl told her partner who was complaining about using one: "It would cut down on your good time and mine a lot more if I got pregnant."

Encouraging your son or daughter to use a condom for protection means realistically talking about the feelings surrounding it, and the barriers that will be in their way. Don't dismiss the barriers too lightly, yet stay on course in getting the point across that condoms are a good and safe method, and the best protection against STDs, no matter how negative their partner may feel about them. Girls have to hear the message that they aren't "bad" to expect a guy to have a condom, they are "smart." Guys have to hear that using a condom is the *only* way they can be certain they are protected from becoming a father before their time.

THE SPONGE

With the renewed interest in nonprescription methods, it was only a matter of time before one of history's oldest methods of contraception would be rediscovered. The sponge in its updated version is a cup-shaped device inserted into the vagina so as to cover the cervix, and consists of a resilient, hydrophilic, polyurethane foam that has a spermicide. It works by releasing the spermicide to kill the sperm, and blocks the path of the sperm.

Its greatest disadvantage is that it carries all of the emotional taboos of the other barrier methods. However, for teens, it has the advantage that it can be inserted hours in advance of intercourse. It is marketed over the counter and is easy to use and disposable.

Although effectiveness rates are still not really solid (because it is so new), it is essentially equivalent to that of the diaphragm.

METHODS THAT ARE BETTER THAN NOTHING AT ALL, BUT NOT BY MUCH

Those listed below are among the least useful for teenage girls because they have to be inserted right before intercourse with all of the same Good Girl/Bad Girl waverings of the condom and sponge, without the effectiveness. The best thing that can be said about foams, creams, and suppositories is that they are available without a prescription.

FOAM

This is an effervescent spermicide that blocks the cervix. Effective rates range from good to lousy. It is very effective when used along with the condom. The problem for teens is that it has to be used right before intercourse. Teens say it is "embarrassing," "messy," and "yucky." There are some indications that the chemical in the foam (nonoxynol-9) does offer some protection against sexually transmitted diseases.

Suppositories

These are small wax pellets, like tampons, that melt a spermicidal chemical when placed near the mouth of the cervix. Teenage girls often get mixed up and buy products for "feminine hygiene" (Norforms, for example) because drugstores usually display everything from contraceptives to vaginal deodorants in the same section.

Periodic Abstinence (Often Called Natural Family Planning)

This method is based on preventing pregnancy by not having intercourse when the woman is fertile. Knowing when you are fertile is difficult for most adult women, and nearly impossible for young women. To find out when she is ovulating, a woman has to chart the dates of her menstrual periods (calendar method), her temperature (basal body temperature method), or changes in her vaginal secretions (cervical mucus method), or some combination of these. The advantage is that it doesn't interfere with the body via chemicals. It can be effective when the couple is highly motivated. The disadvantage is that it takes incredible devotion to keep track of the menstrual cycle, and even then ovulation doesn't happen when it is supposed to. It works a lot better in theory than in practice. However, for those who feel they really prefer a natural method of family planning, there are a number of detailed workbooks available, and trained counselors to help in family planning clinics. (Note: This method is often called the "rhythm" method, but that term is too narrow and not used by family planners.)

WITHDRAWAL

This takes more control than most men, especially teens, can muster under the circumstances, because it involves pulling the penis out of the vagina just before ejaculation, and a few seconds can mark the difference between success and failure. Even if he manages this great feat of self-control, this method doesn't keep all of the sperm from entering the uterus because the pre-ejaculate fluid contains semen. It's not unusual for a teenage guy to achieve orgasm as soon as he enters the girl. He may not want to, and not think he will, but it's a matter of lack of experience in delaying a climax. The other problem is biology: The male has to "pull out" when every nerve in his body is telling him not to. And it's not a satisfactory method for the girl; she is usually too petrified that he won't withdraw in time. And last, but not least, withdrawal has a poor track record: close to thirty pregnancies per hundred women in a year.

DOUCHING

Many teenage girls believe douching with a strong solution, such as vinegar spurted into the vagina right after intercourse, is a method of birth control. Some think using a strong soda pop, like Coca-Cola, works. But no matter what solution is used, you have to stress that douching isn't a method of birth control. Sperm enter the uterus about 90 seconds after a man ejaculates into the vagina. That's fast. And there is the possibility that douching can provide a force to move the sperm into the uterus.

A SUMMARY OF THE FACTS

1. Out of about 5 million teenage girls who are sexually active, close to 3 million obtain effective contraception—oral contraceptives, diaphragms—from family planning clinics or private physicians. Unfortunately, they may stop using it when they break up their sexual relationship, and then not use anything the first few times they have sex with a new partner. Approximately 600,000 girls use spermicides or rely on their partner's use of condoms. Close to 600,000 girls use ineffective methods such as rhythm (not really practicing periodic abstinence, but rather not having sex when they *think* they are fertile), douching, or their partner's withdrawal. *About 800,000 teenage girls use nothing at all.* This adds up to some 1.4 million girls every year at great risk of getting pregnant.
2. During the past five years, however, use of prescription methods among teens has declined. The trend is toward using less effective nonprescription methods, which places these highly vulnerable teenage girls at increased risk of pregnancy.
3. Why teens don't use contraception on a consistent basis or not at all (a summary of a slew of studies):

- They believe it is more romantic when sex just happens, and birth control takes away the spontaneity of the moment.
- They don't think they will get pregnant (teens are notorious risk takers in general).
- They are afraid to go to a clinic or a doctor because they fear their family will find out ("My parents would just die," or "My mom (or dad) would kill me").
- They are embarrassed to go into a store and buy a birth control product—the clerk might disapprove, or they could

run into someone they know or, worse, someone who knows their mom or dad.

- Their partner doesn't want them to use anything.
- Girls fear getting a pelvic exam.
- They can't talk to their partner about it.
- They fear adverse side effects.
- They have had sex a few times and didn't get pregnant (only about 40 percent of teen girls used a method the last time they had sex).
- They don't know much about how to get or how to use birth control.

4. What spurs most teenage girls (nearly four out of ten) to go to a family planning clinic is that they fear they are pregnant.
5. Only about 14 percent of teenage girls seek contraceptives from a clinic before ever having sex.
6. About 8 percent of teenage girls seek contraceptives within three months of first intercourse. The vast majority delay anywhere from three months to a year (the median is nine months).

CHAPTER TEN

THE PROSPECT OF PREGNANCY

THIS ISN'T A PRIMER on teenage pregnancy because, if your teen becomes pregnant, or is involved in a pregnancy, you'll need more information than a chapter in any book can offer (see the special note at the end of this chapter). Rather, I'll arm you with enough solid facts about the dismal script of teenage pregnancy to make a convincing case to your teen about the necessity to avoid it in the first place.

Go directly to the crux of the situation. *Both* sons and daughters need to hear that, no matter how a teenage girl (actually, any woman) solves the problem of finding herself unintentionally pregnant, she will pay a price. There is no such thing as a little bit pregnant; it is one of life's absolutes —she is pregnant or she isn't. Once pregnant, there aren't many options, only three: abortion; delivery and relinquishing for adoption; or delivery and motherhood. A woman can juggle the pros and cons with the man involved, with family, and with friends, or get professional counseling—*but the ultimate decision is hers alone.* Only she can decide her own fate. And what to do about an unintended pregnancy is one of the loneliest and most agonizing decisions a woman can face. If she is thinking about the possibility of abortion, she will have to make up her mind in a matter of a few weeks. A safe, reasonably priced, and easily available abortion must be performed within the first trimester. As for the guy, he can try to persuade her to do what he thinks best about the situation, lend moral and financial support, but, in the end, he is not the one who will make the decision. Even if he feels unable to cope with teenage fatherhood and thinks it would be best if she got an abortion, or put the child up for adoption —but she doesn't agree—it's out of his hands even though his life will be altered. He doesn't have to marry her, but he will be legally responsible for child support: He is a teenage father, whether he wants to be or not.

THE PARENT'S ANGUISH

What about parents? Stand aside. If you are the parent of a daughter who gets pregnant, you can provide support and counseling for her decision, but the final verdict on what to do is hers, even though she is a minor and you are responsible for her. If you are the parents of a son involved in a pregnancy, you will have to anxiously await the girl's decision. Parents can cajole and persuade, but are, in reality, hapless bystanders. All protests to the contrary, a parent can become an unintended grandparent. And it's difficult to be devoid of self-pity, even though you understand that no girl wants to get pregnant unintentionally—it's a mistake, an accident.

I'm sure you don't need convincing about how devastating this can be to a family, emotionally and financially: an all-round heartbreak. But teenagers don't always consider how teen pregnancy, especially if the mother keeps the child, affects other members of a family.

You need to be straightforward. Remind your daughter or son that *no teen is an island* by discussing the *family* dynamics of teenage pregnancy. For instance, share with them the situation of a family where the daughter, who is 17 and not married, is raising her year-old child. Her mother (I'll call her Betty) says, "There are no good solutions to this problem—there are only fly-by-the-seat-of-your-pants, make-do salvaging." Betty gets tearful just remembering how distraught she felt when her daughter told her she was pregnant. Then, Betty and her husband fought over whether to persuade the daughter to have an abortion, or arrange for an adoption. Betty felt they shouldn't pressure her. Her daughter opted to have the baby, and raise the child in her family home. The guy involved wanted nothing to do with the girl or the baby. While Betty is quick to say that the baby is adorable, she admits to being haunted by the feeling she erred in not getting her daughter to seriously consider the life-altering consequences of keeping the child. Betty's marriage is, as she puts it, "in shambles." And her assessment of her daughter's situation is: "She's overwhelmed with the responsibility of the baby and trying to finish high school. Now that the novelty of the baby has worn off, her friends pretty much ignore her. She's depressed almost all of the time because she realizes now that she wasn't ready to be a mother." Betty goes on to say that the rest of the family isn't faring much better: "Her younger sister [age 13] feels humiliated, hostile, and angry, because she feels her sister, 'made a mess out of her life,' and has 'ruined everything for everybody.' "

Betty's grief is echoed in almost every story told to me by a parent of a teenager who got pregnant, especially when family life is stretched in a taut line over the responsibilities of raising the teen's child. Most parents express lingering guilt and confusion about whether they did the right thing in handling the crisis. Even if their daughter's choice (or that of the girl who their son got pregnant) was abortion or adoption, the scars run deep. But when the teen decides to keep the child, many parents and siblings wonder if they will ever be able to work it out.

Your son or daughter may not relate to the stories of other families. So be crystal clear: You, and the other members of the family, have a right to be concerned that an unintended pregnancy doesn't happen. Although an individual is the one who is pregnant and has to deal with it, in reality, and in the end, everyone close to them will have to shoulder the burden. Of course, you will want to tell them that the family would be supportive in the situation of an unintended pregnancy; family love means family solidarity. But a teen has to accept the facts. Their family wouldn't be exactly volunteers, and therefore a teen couldn't expect everyone to pitch in with a willing, happy attitude.

A SUMMARY OF THE FACTS

It's not a pretty picture.

• Teenage pregnancy, "children having children," has reached incredible proportions: in 1980, 562,330 babies were born to teen mothers, half of them to unmarried teenagers, and nearly 10,000 to girls 14 or younger. About 460,120 abortions were chosen by teenage girls. In all, counting estimated miscarriages, there were 1.11 million teen pregnancies in 1980.

• Out-of-wedlock births have tripled between 1960 and 1980. The proportion of teenage girls who got married after (and presumably because) they got pregnant dropped from one in three in 1971 to one in six in 1979. Currently, 40 percent of the teenagers under 18 who gave birth are married; among those under 20, 60 percent are married. But these marriages are unstable: One out of every two teenage marriages ends in divorce within five years.

• About one-third of all abortions each year are obtained by teenagers—about half of these by 18- to 19-year-olds; 45 percent by 15- to 17-year-olds; and 5 percent by those 14 and younger. Several studies show that educational attainment and socioeconomic status are related to the decision to terminate the pregnancy. Those teenage girls who choose an abortion tend to come from families of higher socioeconomic status and have mothers of higher educational levels than those choosing to continue the pregnancy.

• For the teenager, abortion is many times safer than childbearing. Teens risk higher rates of toxemia, anemia, and maternal death than non-teens.

• Mental retardations, birth defects, epilepsy, and birth injuries occur more often among children born to teenage mothers.

• Adoption is not the choice of most pregnant teens. It is estimated that about 3 percent of teenage girls relinquish their baby for adoption (the figure may be as high as 10 or 15 percent since not all adoptions are reported as such). Compare this to 1960, when an estimated 80 percent of all unmarried teen mothers chose adoption.

• Nine percent of teenage mothers attempt suicide. That figure is seven times the national percentage for teenage girls without children who attempt suicide.

• Too often, a teenager having a child becomes a prescription for a life of dependency and poverty. In 1985, one out of every two poor families with children under 18 resides in a home headed by a single mother. More than half of all women on welfare began as a teenage mother.

• Pregnancy is the number one cause of school dropouts among girls; their girlfriend's pregnancy is suspected of being the leading cause of school dropouts among teen boys.

• Although the number of teen births among whites is rising faster than among blacks, black teens are five times as likely to give birth out of wedlock.

• About 50 percent of unmarried pregnant teens become pregnant during the first six months of having sexual intercourse. One out of five teenage pregnancies begins in the first month of having sex. And teens age 15 or younger at the time of *first* intercourse are twice as likely to become pregnant in the first six months of sexual activity than teens who have their first intercourse at the age of 18 or 19.

• Teenage girls under the age of 15 don't readily acknowledge they are pregnant. In one study, only 28 percent realized they were pregnant, and only another 27 percent acknowledged the pregnancy in the second month. After they did acknowledge the pregnancy, only 46 percent began prenatal care during the first trimester. Few of these young teens consider alternatives to having the baby; just 32 percent even considered abortion, and only 20 percent thought about adoption.

• Given the recent statistics on pregnancy by the age of 20, one in ten women will have been pregnant at least once.

• Under the U.S. Supreme Court decision of *Roe* v. *Wade*, 1973, a woman, regardless of her age or marital status, is legally entitled to an abortion during the first trimester of pregnancy. In the second trimester (the middle three months) abortion procedures may be regulated by the state in ways related to maternal health. The decision for abortion remains solely between the woman and her physician. A physician dealing with a minor may request parental consent, or at least notification, but it is not a legal requirement. During the last trimester, the state may regulate or forbid abortion, except in cases where it is necessary to save the life or health of the mother. Parental consultation would be required by almost all physicians.

• Overall, although different adoption policies exist from state to state and from agency to agency, the mother of the child, even if she is a minor, usually does not have to obtain legal parental consent for her to relinquish her child for adoption. Nor can parents force her not to relinquish. However, many adoption agencies, and many courts, are now beginning to request (or require) the written consent of the child's father to the adoption.

• *Teen girls who are strongly committed to educational and occupational achievement are most likely to postpone motherhood until their aspirations are fulfilled.*

A SPECIAL NOTE: If your teen does become pregnant, or is involved in a pregnancy, get immediate help. Typically a teenager is not mature enough to make, unaided, a decision about pregnancy that may affect her life and the lives of others. Teens, when they find out they are pregnant, or find out their girlfriend is pregnant, become paralyzed by indecision and unable to confront the reality of the pregnancy. You may be hindered in your efforts to provide direction because of your own emotional crisis. Counseling is a must, and there are many agencies that offer free or low-cost nonjudgmental counseling. The Yellow Pages list these most often under "Counseling," "Pregnancy Counseling," and "Women's Health Care."

CHAPTER ELEVEN

A FACT OF LIFE: STDs*

DESPITE THE WONDERS OF MODERN SCIENCE, there is a possibility your teen could contract a sexually transmitted disease (STD): One out of seven teenagers does. Moreover, about one out of four people between the ages of 15 and 55 will have an STD at some point in their lives, with 85 percent of these reported STDs in the age group of 15 to 30.

The statistics are awesome, and so are the complications, especially for young women. Teenage girls have a high incidence of PID (pelvic inflammatory disease), which results from untreated sexual infections such as chlamydia and gonorrhea. Aside from the health problems PIDs cause, they can damage the reproductive system and cause infertility or sterility. On top of all that, unlike syphilis and gonorrhea, which once were the only "venereal" diseases that struck fear into our hearts, some of the STDs rampant today don't respond to the easy treatment of antibiotics.

* Teens tend to use the term "VD," or "venereal disease," rather than STD (sexually transmitted disease); however, the latter is the current usage.

The reality is this: Teens need to be educated about STDs even if they haven't had sexual intercourse. The old saying, "An ounce of prevention is worth a pound of cure," is right on target.

FIRST THINGS FIRST

Don't waste time dwelling on "why" people get an STD. It really isn't very mystifying: Sexually transmitted diseases—with the notable exception of some cases of AIDS—are contracted by having sex with someone who has the disease. A critical fact to convey to your teen is this: Anyone who is sexually active can get an STD, and the more sexual partners the greater the chance of being infected.

Let your teen know that the most important action a person can take to prevent getting an STD (aside from not having sexual intercourse) is to practice safe sex, which includes using a condom and contraceptive foam, cream, or jelly; not exchanging what the researchers call "body fluids"—semen or blood; limiting the number of sexual partners; and being as sure as you can be that your partner doesn't have a sexual infection.

Some people say that, with effective vaccines a long way off, the best protection against STDs is to practice that old safeguard, monogamy. For those not in a monogamous relationship, in addition to practicing safe sex, health researchers recommend not having casual sex, because even a discriminating person can't know a new partner's complete sexual history or whether the person has used intravenous drugs in the past eight years. "If you're a single woman, remember: no casual sex again," warns Dr. Helen Singer Kaplan, director of the Human Sexuality Program at New York Hospital–Cornell Medical Center. "Know your partner."

For teenagers, I would sum up the basics in a package.

They need to know how to protect themselves by being discriminating about a sexual partner, by using safe sex precautions, by being aware of the danger signals of STDs, and by taking responsibility to seek treatment if they contract an infection.

THE NEXT STEP

Teens are often overwhelmed with guilt and stunned by panic if they suspect they might have "something." They may worry more about having their parents find out than about the threat to their health. Some try to ignore the problem, hoping with all of their might that it is "nothing" or that it will just "go away." Others simply don't know what to do, or where to go for help. So keep your discussions about STDs on an even keel. Teens need to know that getting an STD isn't a punishment for having sex; it's embarrassing, that's for sure, but it isn't *shameful.*

Convey the importance of prevention, of course, but don't neglect to emphasize the importance of getting treatment to avoid serious consequences. Tell them an examination and lab tests are the only way to be sure you don't have a sexual infection, or to learn what kind of infection you have. Self-diagnosis and self-treatment are very risky. And even if symptoms do go away, the disease doesn't unless medically treated. What is even worse, a person (especially women) can be infected and not know it at all, which brings up an unpleasant side effect of STDs: A person who has a sexual disease must take responsibility for telling their partner(s). As the authors of *Healthy Sex* explain: "It is important to keep in mind that the issue of 'guilt' is less significant than the issue of responsibility; because so many of these infections can be asymptomatic, the buck stops with the person who has the symptoms."

If your son or daughter does contract a sexual infection,

and simply can't bring themselves to inform the person they've had sex with, as a last resort they can give the name of their sexual partner to the Department of Health in your county. A health worker will contact the other person and let them know they have been exposed to an STD and must be tested. In some cases, there is no choice. Clinics and physicians are legally required to report gonorrhea, syphilis, and AIDS to the health department for follow-up (notifying the sexual partner of possible infection). Stress to your teens that health workers are not the police; they work to stop the spread of STDs and to help someone know they are at risk, and they are forbidden, by law, to disclose the name of the person involved. Everything is kept confidential.

Although it may not thrill you, you need to tell your teens that nowhere does a teenager of *any* age need a parent's permission to be treated for a sexual disease. Their privacy is absolutely protected, and many clinics, particularly all health department facilities, are free.

BEING AWARE

I'll give you a general overview of the most common STDs to help you bring up the topic with your teen. But the finer points of many sexual diseases—including other sexual infections not discussed in the next section—are so varied and complicated that it's a good idea to provide your teen with the most current reading material (since research information is updated constantly). I've listed some of these in the resource list in the back of this book.

Don't fret about not knowing all there is to know about the epidemiology of sexual infections. What counts is your being aware of the issue, and letting your son or daughter know they can talk to you about it.

A SUMMARY OF THE FACTS

The following is a brief update on the most common, and the most serious, sexually transmitted diseases passed from one person to another through sexual intercourse or other sexual activity or, in some instances, by close body contact. They are listed in order of the most reported (or estimated) cases to the least reported.

CHLAMYDIA

Chlamydia is the fastest-growing sexual disease in the United States: An estimated 3 to 4 million men and women have contracted it. Although most people haven't heard of it (yet), it is much more common in teenagers than is gonorrhea. The infection is caused by the organism *Chlamydia trachomatis*, and can be known as nonspecific vaginitis in women and nonspecific urethritis in men. It tends to develop slowly and have relatively mild symptoms—characterized by slight pain and some discharge—but women often experience no symptoms at all. Untreated, the organism in women can cause pelvic inflammatory disease (PID), which is likely to result in scarring of the fallopian tubes and infertility, or ectopic (tubal) pregnancy; in men, the organism can cause inflammation of the major sperm-carrying passage from the testes, which could lead to infertility. Another serious consequence of chlamydial infections is that newborn babies, delivered vaginally, can contract the disease from the mother; the newborns can develop conjunctivitis, which can cause blindness, and pneumonia, which can be fatal.

Chlamydia is diagnosed mostly by specialized culture, but recently a simpler, cheaper test has been developed. It is often safer to assume chlamydia through the process of elimination and treat it than to be sorry. Treatment is usually antibiotics, but it's not a "one-shot" deal, because the organism is so persistent that it takes 10 to 14 days of tetracycline or erythromycin to eliminate it.

GONORRHEA

Gonorrhea, also known as the clap, drip, gleet, dose, and others, is caused by gonococcus bacteria. The highest incidence of gonorrhea in the United States is in the 20- to 24-year-old age group, with the 15- to 19-year-olds running a close second; overall, there are 2 million cases a year. Many gonorrhea infections have no symptoms, but when they do they usually appear in men (about 10 percent have no symptoms) two to nine days after exposure: painful urination and an uncomfortable yellowish discharge from the penis. Some women experience vaginal or pelvic discomfort, but about 80 percent of affected women have no early symptoms. Untreated gonorrhea in women can cause PID and as a result sterility. In both men and women, gonorrhea can spread throughout the body affecting joints and even the heart valves. And, like chlamydia, it can be transmitted from a mother's vagina to her infant's eyes during birth and cause blindness.

The diagnosis is by a Gram's stain smear done in a clinic or a doctor's office, but, as it is not always accurate, a bacterial culture is better. Treatment is either antibiotic pills or a penicillin injection.

VENEREAL WARTS

Venereal warts are skin-colored "wartlike" bumps that usually appear around the genitals and sometimes around the anus. They are caused by a virus, and, left untreated, they can multiply rapidly. They are passed from person to person by direct contact, but not everyone that comes in contact with warts will catch them. Still, 1 million new cases are estimated each year. Treatment is removal by chemicals, freezing, or a surgical procedure.

Venereal warts have increasingly been linked to malignancies and premalignant conditions affecting the genitals and the anus. There is a severe consequence to newborns. A pregnant woman with them can transmit the virus to her baby during vaginal delivery; the virus can lodge in the infant's larynx, trachea, and lungs.

HERPES SIMPLEX VIRUS TYPE II

Herpes progenitis, or genital herpes, is caused by the herpes simplex type 2 (HSV-2) virus, which is related to the virus (HSV-1) that causes lesions (cold sores or blisters) on the mouth and lips. An estimated 5 million to 20 million people have genital herpes, with an estimated 500,000 new cases a year. Despite the uproar about HSV-2, most people who have it manage to have satisfactory sex lives and never transmit the disease to another person.

Generally, genital herpes is transmitted through sexual intercourse. The virus is passed by direct contact with lesions, but can be transmitted from one part of the body to another by the hands, especially if the skin is damaged, say, by eczema. Also, there is a possibility of secondary bacterial infections where a blister has been scratched.

Symptoms, which first appear 2 to 20 days (although sometimes they don't show up for several months) after exposure, include tiny painful, fluid-filled blisters on or around the genitals or the anus. Other symptoms may include a general achiness, swollen lymph glands, and a slight fever. While the symptoms usually diminish in a few weeks, once you have been infected the virus persists in the body indefinitely. In genital herpes the virus's "home base" is at the base of the spine; flare-ups occur when the virus travels through nerve branches from the spine to the genital area. Some people never have another active episode, but usually there will be a recurrence from time to time, especially if the person's resistance is low or if they are under emotional stress.

A serious consequence for women is the possible link between HSV-2 and an increased risk of cervical cancer. A special problem with genital herpes is that it can cause herpes encephalitis, a virulent, often lethal brain infection in newborns delivered vaginally to mothers who have an active case of HSV-2.

While there is, as of yet, no cure for genital herpes, antiviral ointments can alleviate symptoms, and may also diminish recurences.

Syphilis

Most people think syphilis has been relegated to the history books, but not so: About 90,000 new cases are reported each year. Syphilis is caused by small, spiral-shaped bacteria that invade the body through a break (no matter how minuscule) in the skin where they enter the bloodstream and attack vital organs. Syphilis is transmitted by direct contact with infected lesions or a rash and is commonly passed on by sexual intercourse.

Left untreated it is a "silent" killer because, although the external symptoms disappear, the disease leads to progressive damage to the heart, liver, nerves, and brain. It causes blindness, paralysis, and insanity. An unborn baby can get syphilis from its infected mother because the disease attacks the fetus through the placenta.

The infection of syphilis progresses in three different stages with long intervening periods when a person is free of symptoms. In the first stage, a *painless* sore or blister called a chancre appears on the body wherever the infection came into contact with injured skin or mucous membrane. In the second stage, there may be many or few symptoms. A rash may appear over the body, particularly on the palms of the hands and soles of the feet. Sometimes the rash appears at the same time the chancre does. It is critical to have syphilis diagnosed in the first and second stages because by the third stage the disease is often incurable.

The problem with early detection is that syphilis is the "great imitator"; the chancre can easily be mistaken for something else, and masking of the second-stage symptoms can occur if the person is taking antibiotics for another sexual infection. Diagnosis of second- and third-stage syphilis can only be done by a blood test—the VDRL—but it's only reliable about seven to ten days after the chancre appears. Secondary syphilis can be diagnosed with 100 percent accuracy. Treatment requires long-term antibiotic therapy and blood tests every three months for a year after the first negative blood test.

AIDS: Acquired Immune Deficiency Syndrome

While a great deal remains to be learned about AIDS, knowledge about it increases almost daily, including a store of information about how to prevent contracting it and transmitting it to others. AIDS is probably caused by a virus (called human T-cell leukemia or HTLV-III/LAV). This virus damages the body's immune system, leaving it vulnerable to many infections or cancers. People don't actually die directly of AIDS, but rather of their inability to combat other diseases.

So far, nearly all cases of AIDS have been reported from four groups of people: homosexual or bisexual males (more than 70 percent of the cases are in these two groups), intravenous drug abusers who share needles (they account for about 17 percent),

Haitian entrants into the United States, and persons with hemophilia who have contracted the disease from AIDS-contaminated blood transfusions. It is as yet unknown how widespread AIDS will become in heterosexuals. Dr. James Curran, director of the CDC Task Force on AIDS, estimates that 10–20 percent of those exposed to HTLV-III/LAV will develop full-blown AIDS, and another 20 percent will develop AIDS-related complex, which may or may not mean they develop AIDS. Some people exposed to AIDS never get it themselves, but become "carriers" and can expose others to the virus.

On a positive note, AIDS does not appear to be transmitted by casual contact. Evidence suggests that AIDS is transmitted through "an exchange of bodily fluids," especially blood or semen, and, perhaps, but to a lesser degree, saliva. Symptoms of AIDS are also symptoms of minor illnesses like colds or flu, only they keep coming back or don't go away at all. Other symptoms in addition to a general malaise can include unexplained weight loss, recurring fever and/or night sweats, swollen lymph glands, unusual blemishes on the tongue or mouth, and red to purple or blue raised patches on the body. Diagnosis is made by clinical and laboratory tests. Radiation, interferon, and chemotherapy have been used to diminish the infections or cancers, but so far there is no cure for AIDS; eventually the body is overwhelmed and the person dies (fewer than 10 percent of persons with AIDS have survived longer than three years).

Since AIDS was first recognized as a disease by the Center for Disease Control in 1981, diagnosed cases have doubled every five to nine months. Meade Morgan, chief statistician for the federal anti-AIDS program, says, "There is not yet a sign of a plateau," but the alarming speed with which the disease spread in its early months apparently has slowed down. Hopeful signs are on the horizon: Researchers are seeing major changes in homosexual men's sexual practices and predict these changes probably will lead to a leveling off of the spread of the disease. And, the Public Health Service is committed to the goal of stopping the transmission of AIDS by the year 2000. But for now, millions of Americans, straight and gay, are at risk. Most of the heterosexual population has yet to get that message. Get in touch with your public health department for the most up-to-date information.

EPILOGUE

IT'S ALL WORTH IT

I've talked at length about the warmth and pleasure you'll experience communicating with your daughter or son about what really matters about love, sex, and relationships. Want to know how kids feel about it? Hear what three young adults had to say about how much those moments meant to them.

One of my university students was reminiscing about his early youth: "When I was about 15, I was a real smart-ass. One day hanging out at my house I was flaunting the fact that I captured the best-looking girl in school to my buddies. After they split, my mom asked me to sit down at the kitchen table and listen up a minute. My mom said something to me (she hadn't said much 'personal' to me before) that's stuck with me ever since: 'You are the first boy Kimberley has ever gone with. This gives you a special place in her life. I remember the first boy I fell in love with. He is etched in my heart forever. And I feel happy thinking about the good times we shared. I'm sure he feels the same about me. I hope you and Kimberley will cherish the memory of each other in the years to come, too. Be sure you end up respecting each other so she, as well as you, will always have a good feeling about loving another person.' I felt so close to my mom at that moment. And it brought us closer together about everything. I know it all happened because she cared enough to straighten me out. It may sound odd, but something else changed for me. I began to see and respect her not just as a 'mom' but as a very terrific person."

A woman in her early twenties told me of a "turning point" in her relationship with her parents when she was 16. She had gotten home way after curfew, and her parents were waiting up. "I started to make some contrived excuse and promise to 'never be late again,' when my mom and dad sat down on each side of me and gave me a big hug. They asked me if I wanted to talk about why I couldn't get home on time. They were upset all right, but acted more concerned than mad. I just opened up and told them that I had been parking wth Sam (my date), and we were necking like crazy. Then, things got more intense and we almost had sex. I was scared as hell. They were *very* understanding, and talked about how wonderful it feels to kiss someone you care for, and how easy it is to go from necking to sex, because passion is a powerful feeling. I shouldn't feel ashamed. And they said I would know more in the future about how to avoid getting into difficult situations and would be better able to handle my own feelings. It was a real relief to know they still loved me, and were on my side. Although we had a lot of talks about a lot of things over the years, I've always treasured that night because I learned I could be really honest and open with them."

Looking back two years before, a 19-year-old woman recalled: "One day my dad had to take me over to my girlfriend's house. While we were driving, he said that Jim (the guy I was going with) was a great guy, and he could see why I liked him so much. He just kept looking at the road but I could see him glance at me when he didn't think I was looking. Very quietly, he told me, 'Love is something very special. When it leads to sex you have to be very careful about not being blinded by it.' He didn't put me on the defensive, nor ask me if I had sex. Just very matter-of-factly he gave me the facts about the importance of preventing an unwanted pregnancy, because, as he said, 'an unwanted pregnancy can wreck a lot of lives.' I know how hard it was for him to bring that up. I'm sure he didn't approve of me having sex, but he didn't make me feel cheap, guilty, or too stupid to understand what he meant. It really hit me, because Jim and I were having sex, and I was too shy to do anything about birth control. I admired Dad for having the courage, and the tact, to make me think about what I was doing. And it made me realize how lucky I am to have a dad that is so caring."

Those experiences, and many more like them, make it very clear that a warm touch communicates beyond mere words. And isn't it wonderful, and fortifying, to know that your loving concern and honesty will be remembered by your son or daughter long after they have left the nest?

PRACTICE SESSIONS

Here are the most commonly asked questions I've had from teens along with a sample of how I usually respond to them. My answers here are very brief, and clearly not the best or the only way to respond to the questions. Remember, I'm not trying to put words in your mouth. Also, refer back to the chapter indicated for more details.

You might want to cover up my suggested responses before you read them. Practice what you would say. Then you can compare and contrast my answer with yours. Hopefully, between the two of us, the responses will cover all bases.

Chapter Three: Teenagers, aka Adolescents

Q. Why are some boys' penises bigger than others?
A. Because everyone's body is shaped uniquely and, just like ears, noses, and hands, a penis is a part of the body.

You really can't tell much about the size of a penis by looking at it when it's in the flaccid state (soft). Some penises erect to sizes larger than others from the flaccid state. The size does not matter, because size has nothing to do with giving or having sexual satisfaction.

Q. Why do boys tease girls about their breasts? Do you think a girl should ignore them, or punch them out?

A. Boys seem to go through periods of trying to get attention from girls any way they can. And, unfortunately, in our society some men feel they have the right to comment on a woman's breast size, shape, whatever. Try to see it as their problem, not yours. But you don't have to put up with feeling uncomfortable when they tease you. Don't lose your temper (they'll tease you even more). And don't giggle: that gives boys the idea you are enjoying being teased. Just look them straight in the eye, and say something like, "Grow up," or "That is *so* boring." Eventually, they will leave you alone because you have given them the direct message that they can't get your goat.

Q. Does a girl lose a lot of blood during her period? Does it make them weaker during "that time of the month"?

A. Menstruation is a perfectly normal function of a girl's body. It doesn't make girls weak. Menstruation happens when the built-up lining (the endometrium) of the uterus, a combination of blood vessels and tissue (it isn't needed when there is no fertilized egg to nourish), is sloughed off by the uterus and discharged through the vagina over several days. It is a cleansing process, a sign that a girl's body is functioning normally. On the average, the total discharge during the four or five (or more) days of menstruation is only about four ounces of blood, and that happens a little at a time.

Q. What is a wet dream?

A. A wet dream (nocturnal emission) occurs when a boy becomes sexually aroused in his dreams and has an ejaculation. He may not even wake up at that time because the ejaculation happens spontaneously. Wet dreams are very normal—the body's way of developing the male's capacity to someday father children.

Q. I'm 15 and the only one of my friends that hasn't started her period. When do you think it will happen?

A. Every girl begins her period when her body is ready. Some girls menstruate at 11, others at 16, even at 17. You're on your own biological clock. But if you are still concerned in a few months or so, you might see a clinician for a checkup.

Q. I have a friend named John. He's got pubic hair. I'm taller than he is, but I'm bald. Is something wrong with me (we are both the *same* age, 13)? Or is something wrong with him?

A. Both of you are normal. John is going through sexual development according to his body's time clock and you are going through it according to yours. This means you'll get pubic hair when your body is ready—any day now.

Q. How many sperm does it take to fertilize a female egg?

A. One.

Chapter Four: What Is This Thing Called Love?

Q. How can you tell if you are really in love?

A. Love is a friendship sparked by sexual chemistry. It is quiet understanding, mutual caring, loyalty, and settles for less than perfection. It is a creative force that releases a lot of energy. You feel motivated to be a part of the world around you and want to share your ideas and enthusiasm with your partner. Try this simple test. Take a newspaper and a magazine and see how many items you feel like clipping to talk about with the person you love. If you don't have much in common, or feel lukewarm about discussing ideas and events with him or her, it might be that you are more attracted to the other person than in love. And ask yourself: Do you enjoy each other's company when you are together? Do you really like each other? When you are really in love, you care for the person more and more as you get to know them. If you can share good times and a keen interest in the other person through any number of trials and tribulations around the calendar a few times, it probably is a relationship that will last.

Q. What exactly does it mean to be infatuated with someone? Can't that turn into real love?

A. Infatuation is when you are very attracted to someone but you don't really know them all that well. You feel "crazy" about them, dream about them, and think about them all the time. It is usually marked by a constant state of anxiety and insecurity about what you are feeling and what they are feeling. It drains your energy. You feel tired out most of the time by all of this tension. You argue a lot. Sometimes you feel jealous whenever they express an interest in doing something without you whether you want to do it or not. You wonder if they are "in love" with you all of the time. You feel suspicious about the other person's commitment to you and do a lot of checking up on where they are and who they are with.

One clue for knowing if what you are feeling is infatuation, or something more, is whether being with the person is better than being apart. If being together is more of a drag than your fantasy of what it will be like when you are not together—it's not the genuine thing.

Infatuation doesn't usually turn into a mutually loving, long-lasting relationship because it's based on wishful thinking, not who you really are and who they really are.

Q. How can you get someone to love you that you love?

A. You can't. Love is mutual; the person cares for you because that is how they feel. It's impossible to make someone feel something they don't. Try to develop a friendship with the person you are attracted to, but don't expect it to turn into anything else.

Q. What is the difference between liking and loving someone? I don't mean when the person is a friend, but when they are a boyfriend.

A. The two feelings really differ mostly in intensity. Liking someone usually means that you care for them, enjoy being with them, and they feel the same about you. Loving means you feel all of these same feelings, but the relationship between the two of you is more intense. An added ingredient in loving someone is that you are sexually attracted to them, you feel the need to be close to them, to kiss, to touch.

Q. Is it true that guys don't fall in love as easily as girls, or do they just not show it openly?

A. Boys fall just as hard in love as girls do. Unfortunately, many boys have been taught that to show loving affection or admit to being in love is a weakness, not manly. It is hard for boys to express their loving feelings for all of those reasons. But that doesn't mean they don't feel them; they do.

Q. Is it really impossible for people our age (from a guy in high school) to be in love? I don't mean puppy love, or being crazy about someone, but *in* love.

A. Yes, you can be in love. However, it may be a love for now, not forever. People call young love "puppy love," but that's not really fair. What you feel is real enough, so enjoy it for as long as it lasts. Just don't count on your relationship or your feelings not changing—they are likely to shift as you continue to change yourself. It's great to lose your heart, just don't lose your head.

A CASE STUDY

Now, here is a situation for you to consider with respect to how you might respond.

> Carla, a 15-year-old, says: "Jenny, my best girlfriend, has been going with this cute guy named Paul for two months. She says she loves him and he told her he loves her. Lately, Paul has been coming on to me. He hangs around my locker and calls me every night just to joke around. I didn't start this, but I guess I do like him a lot. He and Jenny broke up today and everyone *blames* me. They say I took Paul away from her. He told my friend Emily that he doesn't love Jenny anymore, and he wants to go with me. But he didn't tell me that. I didn't know he was going to break up with her. What should I do? It's not fair for them to be down on me for something I didn't do. Jenny won't even speak to me."
>
> One approach you might take in talking to her: "Carla, most guys and girls, when they are your age, do fall in and then out of love a lot—it's part of growing up. No one can 'take' someone away from someone else. But ask yourself, 'Did I want Paul to want to go with me? Did I give him any signals that I was interested in him?' Whether it makes sense or not, usually the 'deal' is that, when someone is going with someone, friends are expected to honor 'hands off.' Don't

gloss over your actions if you did encourage Paul. Be honest with yourself. But no matter how you acted, it is really Paul's decision about whom he likes and whom he doesn't. Now, here are some things you can do. Tell Jenny you want to still be friends and you are sorry she feels hurt about the breakup with Paul. Then, you can decide to go with Paul if he does want to do that and that's how you feel about him, but don't expect Jenny or your other friends to approve. Or you can forget about Paul as a boyfriend and continue the friendship the way it was. You may lose Jenny as a friend (at least for a while) whether or not you and Paul start to go together. Don't pick Jenny over Paul, or Paul over Jenny, just to keep someone else happy. You'll have to decide what's more important to you and add up the pluses and minuses."

Chapter Five: What Is Sex? I Mean Really!

Q. How does a person know when they are ready for sex?

A. That depends on so many things, but most people under age 16 aren't ready for all the consequences of having sex. Beyond that age, listen to your inner voice. If you don't feel ready, you aren't. But if you feel confused about what you feel and are having a hard time sorting out what to do, ask yourself these questions:

- Do you feel pressured by a specific person, or by your friends?
- What do you hope to get out of it?
- Will you feel guilty?
- Are you ready to use birth control?
- Could you handle it if the person you have sex with loses interest in you, or talks about it to other people?
- Is having sex a way to prove something (lose virginity) or a way of showing you are a man?

• Are you trying to "get back" at someone—a friend, a teacher, or your parents—for some reason?

Being "not ready" doesn't mean that you're not sexually normal. A lot of teens don't want to be rushed into something they have a lot of reservations about. You have the right to say no, to postpone having sex *just because that's the way you feel.* So don't have sex just because of the pressure. Wait until *you* feel that the person and the situation are right for you.

Q. Why do people have sex?
A. Sexual feelings are a normal and natural combination of strong physical and psychological desires. Because sex is the way humans reproduce, we are biologically programmed to have sexual intercourse. But there isn't any one reason why people have sex. For some, it is the physical expression of close, intense feelings for another person and a pleasurable way to share being loving and intimate. Depending upon a person's needs or moods, having sex fulfills a physical urge for sexual satisfaction. Or people have sex in the hope of having a baby. Because sex is an experience between two people, each brings their own unique personality and feelings about themselves and about their partner into the relationship. Each person may have very different reasons for having sex, and different expectations about what having sex means.

Q. What does an orgasm feel like?
A. It feels different for each person, but generally people say it feels like a lot of intense sexual pleasure quickly followed by a release of tension. The whole body responds, and, after orgasm, you feel sexually satisfied, calm, sometimes sleepy. But, even for the same person, orgasms are not all alike; some are more intense than others.

Q. Do girls get horny, or just boys?

A. Girls can get horny, or want to have sex, just as much as boys. Usually, boys are under more pressure to be assertive about wanting to have sex. And girls worry a lot more than boys do about a pregnancy happening or getting labeled "loose" or "sleazy." So it may appear that girls have less sexual desire than boys, but they don't.

Q. Is it okay to have sex if you really love the person?

A. Yes, if that's what you feel is right for you. (I would also add the responses to the first question.)

Q. If you make love before you're married, does that mean you are bad for the rest of your life?

A. No, having sex before marriage doesn't make a person bad, not for now, and not for the rest of their life. Probably you have heard that sex before marriage is immoral. Not everyone believes that. But if you feel that way, then postpone having sex until you marry. Don't go around feeling guilty about the past, or do something you'll feel guilty about. Having a sexual relationship is a personal decision; stick to your *own values*. By the way, everyone makes mistakes, or does things they wish they hadn't. It's the way humans are.

Q. If you have sex, and it turns you off, will it last forever?

A. Sometimes the reason a person doesn't find sex satisfying is that their partner didn't understand how to make love while having sex. Or you weren't feeling all right about having sex with that person in that situation. Having sex that isn't a good experience doesn't mean sex never will be. It means that, the next time you decide to have a relationship that includes sex, you need to be more selective about whom and when. And it's best you wait until you have a good solid relationship and can communicate your feelings with him or her.

Q. Does masturbating hurt you? Is it all right?

A. Masturbating is perfectly normal. It's really good for you. It's one way to relieve sexual tension and understand how your body responds sexually. Some religions preach against it and call it immoral or depraved, but they are off base. Don't worry about it. Almost everyone has masturbated, and many people consider it to be an important part of their sexual lives. It is perfectly natural. Just do it in private.

Q. What's the difference between "making love" and "having sex"?

A. There's isn't any real difference, physically. A difference might be in the motive or intentions a person has. For example, in "making love," a person could be wanting to express loving feelings as well as sexual desire; in "having sex," the focus might be on having a release from sexual tension or on the pleasure of giving and receiving sexual pleasure.

Q. How can you tell a person (you really like) that you don't want to have sex with them, without hurting their feelings or losing them?

A. Be gentle, but straightforward. Simply say you care for them, but you aren't ready to have sex. You don't have to be defensive or offer a ton of reasons. Just tell them that now is not right *for you*. If the other person cares about you as the unique person you are, they won't pressure you. If they can't honor your feelings and your decision to wait, you have learned a lot about them—they weren't someone worth being close with.

Chapter Six: Relationships and Such

Q. At what age is it okay to start dating?

A. Depends on what you mean by dating and how ready you feel to be with someone as a "date." Usually it's best to take one step at a time. Start out by going out with a group of people. When someone special comes along and you want to go out with them—just the two of you—you'll have more self-confidence and not be all uptight.

Q. How can you tell if a girl will go out with you?
A. You can get a clue from the way she acts toward you. Does she seem to enjoy talking to you? Is she friendly? Is she interested in the same things you are? Stand back and try to figure out her personality. Some girls love to flirt for the fun of it and some girls are really too shy to show they are interested in you. So, how about taking it one step at a time? Do something very casual together—maybe get a Coke after school with a group of friends? Or work on a class assignment? Try spending a little time with her without the pressure of being on a date. That way you'll find out two things: whether *you* really want to go out with her and, by getting to know her a little, whether she wants to go out with you.

Q. How can you tell a guy you don't want to go out with him without hurting his feelings?
A. Be tactful and be direct. Tell him you like him as a friend (if you do), but you aren't interested in him as a date. Don't make up excuses. Lying to spare his feelings only ends up with you feeling guilty for weaving a web of fibs and it makes it more difficult for him to get the message.

Q. Is it okay for people to go out with more than one person at a time?
A. Yes, unless you have made a promise to a person not to date anyone else. If that is the case, and you want to go out with other people, be honest about your feelings—let the other person know you have changed your mind. Going out with different people is a big help toward knowing who you are and learning about what you like and don't like in

another person. Don't date one person exclusively until that is really what *you* choose to do. If the other person pressures you, or threatens never to see you again if you go out with other people, they aren't showing you that they care about what you want and need. Don't expect the person who wants you to date only them to easily go along with a new agreement. But if they can't accept it, that's their choice.

Q. What do you do if you're bored by the relationship with your boyfriend/girlfriend but have nothing better to do?

A. Get off your duff—there is a big world out there. Don't let yourself continue to be tied down to someone after your interest has waned. Move on. Get together with your friends. If they don't want to do anything, find some people who do. Join a club. Go bowling, swimming, play card games. Volunteer to work on a project at school. Before you know it, you'll have something better to do.

Q. Why do girlfriends/boyfriends get so jealous that they don't want you to have any friends?

A. Probably they feel very insecure and are afraid they will lose you if you have other interests. Or maybe they don't find it so easy to make friends. Although you can talk about their feelings, don't give in to them, because not having any friends (guys, girls) cuts you off from a big slice of what is important in life. Don't let anyone control you when it comes to having friends. Don't be intimidated. If they really care for you, they will understand how you feel about having friends. If they don't, they aren't worth the sacrifice.

Q. My girlfriend/boyfriend always wants to be alone with me. We went to a party and she/he got mad because I danced with other people. Should I have

spent the whole party with her/him? Is she/he wrong or am I wrong?

A. Neither of you is right or wrong. It sounds as if you had different ideas about what would happen when you went to a party together. You need to clear up any misunderstandings before you go out again to save any hard feelings. It's a lot more fun to go to a party where everybody dances with everybody. Your girlfriend/boyfriend may be feeling a little insecure about your relationship. So be clear that, although you really like her/him, you don't intend not to have fun with other people.

Q. Why do a lot of girls feel the guy should be the one to pay for everything on a date? I don't mean a special deal, like a prom, but just when you go out?

A. When two people like each other and want to date, they need to work out how the cost of dating will be handled. Going dutch simply makes sense. But you have to look at your situation. As a rule, guys usually are able to earn more money than girls. If possible, girls can offer to share half of the dating expense, at least most of the time. If it isn't possible, look for some other alternatives. A couple could take turns paying for a date, or when she is able she can "foot the bill." The problem with "going dutch" is really less a money matter than a social one. Some guys have been taught that their manhood is at stake if they aren't paying; their egos demand they be in charge, in control. Some girls think that if a guy is willing to spend money on them it is a sign that "he cares," or that paying for a date is the male's obligation for having the pleasure of their company. Hogwash.

Q. When is it okay to start going steady/going together?

A. That depends on how ready you feel, and how serious you take it. Mostly, it's better to wait until you have gone out with a lot of different people. You'll know more about what you are feeling and have some comparisons about people you like. Remember, if you go steady, you may want to break up someday, and breaking up can be very hard to do. You might be better off being close and going together but keeping things casual.

Chapter Seven: Surviving a Broken Heart

Q. Why does a guy say he loves you so much, then the next day breaks up? You'd think they do that just to hurt you.

A. Maybe the guy was only using "love" words because he wanted to be sexually involved. Or maybe at the time he thought he did love you, but by the next day he realized he was in over his head. Sometimes guys say "love" when they mean "like." I don't think guys act that way to hurt girls—they often don't understand how to communicate with girls. Look at it this way: You've learned something important—love takes time and is something felt by both people. Maybe you were too quick to feel you loved him. Next time go slow and don't believe a guy "loves" you by what he says, look at how he acts. And you won't know how he acts until you have know him for a while.

Q. What if you go with a guy and at first you always want to be with him a lot, but after a while you want to pull away because you are afraid of getting so close. But you don't want to hurt the other person. What should you do?

A. What do you mean by "too close"? Physically? Emotionally? Maybe your intuition is telling you that you aren't ready for an intimate relationship. Or do you worry that you will be vulnerable to being hurt if you allow yourself to really care and be close? Talk about your feelings with him. It will help clear the air for both of you.

Q. Why do girls/guys ignore you after you've broken up?

A. Usually, the reason the other person "ignores" you is because they are feeling hurt and don't want to be in a position of being rejected again. Or they may feel embarrassed about being rejected. Sometimes they are uncomfortable around you because of the tension that might have occurred when the relationship was breaking up. Try to see things from their point of view. And keep being friendly. Eventually, they may be receptive to being friends again.

Q. How can you break up without causing too much pain for the other person?

A. Breaking up is always painful, but you can make it easier all around by following these rules:

- One, explain your feelings in person; it's a whole lot kinder than writing a note or telling them on the telephone.
- Two, be firm but gentle and tactful. Don't waffle. It's better to make a clean break than to drag it out.
- Three, be fair. Don't try to skirt around the point or pick a fight so you won't feel guilty about wanting to break up.

Tell the other person you hope you will continue to be friends, that no one is to blame—it's simply time for you to make a change.

Q. What do you do when you're really good friends with a guy and he wants to go out with you, and you *know* it'll ruin your relationship and friendship if you break up?

A. Tell him you value his friendship and you don't want *anything* to ruin it. You would rather have things stay the way they are between you than to muddy the waters by changing your relationship. But before you say anything to him, ask yourself if you are attracted to him (as he obviously is to you). If you are, go ahead and go out. Are you worried about caring about him and then being rejected? Sort out what you really feel about him. If you're not attracted to him, you are wise not to go out with him because chances are if you break up as lovers your friendship won't survive. And a friendship is a rare and wonderful relationship.

Q. What is the best way to get over someone you *really,* really like and you were dating for a real long time? And she won't even speak to you anymore?

A. First of all, everyone feels bad when they break up. It's hard to accept the fact that she doesn't want to go with you anymore. But the sooner you can accept it, the freer you will be to find someone else. Don't blame yourself or feel you were inadequate. Don't play the breaking-up scene over and over in your mind, trying to fix blame. Think about what was right, and take pleasure in that.

Although she isn't speaking to you right now, with a little time she might come around. Maybe she is uncomfortable or embarrassed about what happened. Give her some space; don't come on too strong when you see her, and hopefully you can be friends again.

When you feel you have put her behind you, go out and meet some new people. You'll find someone whom you like and who likes you.

Q. What should someone do if they hear that their boyfriend/girlfriend is thinking about breaking up, but so does the other one, and no one says anything to the other about breaking up?

A. Be brave. Discuss the situation. Don't wait around for "something" to happen. Get it out in the open.

Q. I broke up with a girl last year. Now, I'm flipping out again for her. How can I explain this, without hurting the girl I'm going steady with? I really like her and I don't want to mess it up. What should I do?

A. Well, it sounds like you need to stop going steady. It's not fair to your steady girl (or to yourself) to be with her while you are interested in someone else. You need to tell her you don't want to go steady, that you want to be able to date other people. Be fair and honest. You may be able to part as friends, but don't count on it.

Q. Why do friends stick their noses into it when a couple breaks up? It seems everybody has to take sides. And then her friends won't speak to him, and the other way around. How can you tell your friends to butt out?

A. Friends, most of the time, get involved because they want to demonstrate their loyalty to their buddy. Sometimes friends can't resist being a part of the situation because it beats, well, talking about civics. Or they might be acting out the notion that bad-mouthing one of the couple is *expected* of them because they have to "stick up" for their friend. If you are ever in this situation, tell your friends you appreciate their support, but you don't want them to take sides. And if they say something bad about the other person, tell them very firmly that you don't want to hear it. If you are a bystander, resist the temptation to join in when others are critical of another person involved in a breakup. If you are too shy to speak up, walking away or changing the subject will show that you are not comfortable with this kind of chatter.

Q. How do you get someone to love you again when they say they want to split?

A. You can't. There's no way to "make" anyone love you.

The more you try, the more the other person backs away. It's hard to accept, but love that isn't mutual gets a hard edge over time. It can hurt more than breaking up before things get bitter. Acknowledge that this relationship has come to an end. The sooner you face it, the sooner you can find another and better relationship.

A CASE STUDY

While talking to a large group of teens, I received the following note: "I've been together with a girl for six months. Everything has been great. Until lately. When I call her, she says she is busy and has to run. I was over at her place one night for an hour and all we did was watch TV. She acted kinda funny. I asked her if something was wrong, and she said no, she just had a lot of homework. Then, we were supposed to go to a party at my church last night. I went over to her house to pick her up, and she wasn't there. So I went back home, and called her. She still wasn't there. I left three messages with her mom. She never called me back last night, or this morning. What do you think I ought to do?"

I read the note out loud, and decided to turn to the experts for advice. Here are some of the most typical responses (remember to practice what you would say before you read what they had to say):

> MALE, 18 YEARS OLD: "He shouldn't push it with her. He should ease off of her and make it less uncomfortable and maybe she wouldn't break dates. This would make both of them feel better and maybe pay off later in the long run."

> FEMALE, 16 YEARS OLD: "I would advise him to try talking to her. If she didn't want a relationship, she could at least tell him what she's feeling instead of 'dodging' him. He needs to know so he can go on with his life with or without her."

FEMALE, 16 YEARS OLD: "He shouldn't call or look for her. Wait until he sees her again, and then talk to her about the things she is doing. He should confront her and discuss their problems. If she continues to do it after he's told her how it makes him feel, he should take a good look and see if their relationship is for the best."

MALE, 16 YEARS OLD: "I'd tell him she isn't worth his time. He deserves someone better than her. There is someone out there for him that would treat him better. Drop her."

Chapter Eight: Homosexuality/Homophobia

Q. What does homosexual mean? Is it the same thing as gay?

A. The word *homosexual* comes from the Greek word *homo* meaning "same." It is often used as an adjective, as in homosexual bar, homosexual life-style. Mostly it is used as a noun to describe people who have a preference for a sexual relationship with a person of the same sex over a significant period of time. "Gay" is a synonym for homosexual and some people feel it sounds less judgmental or that it makes a political statement of pride. Other people, including men and women with a sexual preference for partners of the same sex, feel uncomfortable with the word *gay* and prefer to use the term "homosexual." All of this means that pinning a label on a person on the basis of sexual preference is controversial and risky at best.

Q. Why aren't homosexual women called "gay"?

A. Sometimes homosexual woman *are* called "gay" because that word means the person prefers homosexuality rather than heterosexuality. However, many people use the term "lesbian" because it specifically refers to women who choose to have women as their sexual partners. Others don't like either term. Again, labeling other people is very tricky.

Q. What makes a person a homosexual?

A. There are a lot of ideas about why a preference for a sexual partner of the same gender develops in some people and not in others—but that's all they are: ideas. No one knows what "causes" homosexuality.

Sometimes young people wonder if they are homosexual because they have experimented sexually with someone of the same sex. Or they wonder whether having strong sexual feelings for a friend of the same sex means they are, or could be, gay. Most people of both sexes have had the same feelings or were involved sexually with someone of the same sex, in some form or another, while growing up. It's not unusual at all. But it doesn't mean a person is, or will be, homosexual. All I can tell you with any certainty is that knowing whether or not a person prefers a partner of the same or opposite sex is usually, but not always, apparent by the time a person becomes a young adult. Because teens go through so many changes, most experts say that people should wait until they are adults before they make any firm declarations about their true sexual orientation.

Q. What does AC/DC mean?

A. AC/DC describes two types of electric current and is a slang term for bisexuality. Bisexuals are people who can enjoy sex with either same-sex or opposite-sex partners. For some people it is an occasional experiment; for others it isn't. Most often people who have bisexual experiences have a preference for one gender, but that is not necessarily always the case.

Q. Is it true that you can always tell when a person is homosexual?

A. No. The only way to know is when someone tells you they are. There are a lot of misguided ideas that you can "tell" if a man is gay by his appearance (feminine, limp-wristed, lisping, sways back and forth when he walks), and women, too—by their short hair, male clothing, and masculine ("butch") characteristics (deep voice, doesn't flirt, doesn't wear makeup). While it is true that a number of homosexual men may behave in an effeminate way and some homosexual women may behave and look "butch," the vast majority look no different and act no differently than heterosexuals. Those stereotypes are not just off base, they are a way of putting down a group of people who travel on a different path than the majority. It's ridiculous to think that all homosexual persons are alike or act a certain way.

Q. Why are people so cruel to gay people—calling them faggots and queers or always trying to start fights with them?

A. People who tease, mock, or harass gays either are ignorant about homosexuality; are, sadly, trying to find a way of being superior to other people; or are motivated to stamp out something too close for comfort. The irrational hostility and fear many people have toward homosexuality can be described in a word: homophobia. It's a sure sign that the taunter is lacking in self-assurance and self-esteem. No matter what the reasons are behind their cruelty, they need to be told they are out of line. If their peers can't do it, I suggest a teacher or counselor.

Q. Do homosexuals ever become straight and vice versa?

A. Not really. Most of the researchers say a person's sexual orientation is an inherent part of the total self and isn't a choice, but is deeply felt. But sometimes a person, especially while growing up, isn't really exclusively homosexual or heterosexual, and it's not until they reach adulthood that their sexual identity becomes clear. Some people don't discover or accept their preference for the same sex until after they have been in a heterosexual relationship—even marriage. This doesn't mean they were "straight" and then became "gay"; their true sexual orientation was there all along.

Chapter Nine: Hmmm, What about Contraception?

Q. How old does a girl have to be before she can use the pill?

A. She has to be old enough to have established regular menstrual periods. Also, there are many kinds of pills (oral contraceptives). The decision on whether a girl should use a method of oral contraceptive is best made after a medical checkup and after she considers all the options available.

Q. Why is it always the girl who has to use birth control?

A. Ideally, both the guy and the girl should share in the responsibility to prevent her from getting pregnant. And many guys do take the responsibility by using a condom or by helping their partner to use a method effectively and supporting her by going with her to get a method and when she has to have exams and checkups. But that's not all guys. And female biology being what it is, the girl has more at stake in making sure she is protected. It doesn't make sense to take any risk about getting pregnant because it is a hassle or because it isn't fair. It does make sense for a girl to be in charge of her own body.

Q. How does withdrawal work? (A lot of guys say they do it and their girlfriends haven't gotten pregnant.)

A. Withdrawal means that the penis is withdrawn from the vagina before the man ejaculates. It is better than doing nothing, but not by much. It isn't very reliable because it requires a lot of self-control on the part of the guy when his body is compelling him to go on to climax. And it causes frustration and worry for both of the partners that he might not withdraw in time. Also, the semen that seeps out of the penis before ejaculation is loaded with sperm. And when you think about the fact that roughly 40 billion sperm may be produced in each ejaculation you can see why withdrawal doesn't work and why it's risky business. Your friends have been lucky so far. Chances are pretty good they will end up getting their girlfriends pregnant unless they begin using a method of contraception.

Q. What is the best method of birth control for girls?

A. That depends so much on the girl, so it makes sense to learn about how contraception works. (Go back to Chapter 9 and review the methods with your son or daughter or encourage them to visit a family planning clinic or ask a health teacher for information about all the methods available.)

Q. If you take the pill for a long time, does that mean you won't get pregnant later on?

A. No. There are many kinds of pills (oral contraceptives), and a clinician prescribes the best one based on the individual's needs and monitors the client's health. You may have known or heard of someone who was on the pill and then had a difficult time getting pregnant, but that's rare. And usually there are other reasons for her difficulty than having taken the pill.

Q. Can you get pregnant if you have sex the day after your period?

A. A girl can get pregnant at any time. Although there are only a few days each month a girl can conceive, it is really difficult to know exactly when that is—ovulation is supposed to take place midway between periods, but it can occur before, during, or right after a period. Even women who have regular periods can't be sure when they are ovulating. Ovulation can happen at odd times, when under a lot of stress, or when ill, or when your schedule changes (when traveling, for example).

Q. Can a rubber break?
A. Yes. But if it's used properly, chances are it won't.

Q. How can you tell a guy he needs to use a condom?
A. Be direct. Tell him you believe in having safe sex or not having sex. If he won't use one, he is showing he doesn't care enough about you to protect you from getting pregnant. Even if it's hard to do, insist upon it. You'll be glad you did: No one is worth the risk of getting pregnant or contracting an STD.

Q. Is it a hassle going to a birth control clinic? Do they tell your parents? (Note: I grant you that your teen probably won't ask you this question, but I wanted you to know this is one I get all the time, and let you see how I respond to it.)
A. It might be a little trouble getting there, but it's worth it. Clinics welcome everyone who comes, their fees depend on how much you can afford to pay, and their services are confidential. If you aren't ready to consider contraception, you could go there for information and counseling. They leave it up to you to let your parents know if you receive their services.

Q. Is it true that you can't get pregnant if you don't have an orgasm?
A. No, that's not true. All it takes to get pregnant is for one sperm to enter the ovum (the egg), and that can happen even when the woman doesn't have an orgasm.

A CASE STUDY

Here is a situation for you to consider. What advice could you give Judy?

Judy is 16 years old, and her boyfriend, Sammy, is 19. She says, "My boyfriend and I love each other very much. He wants to have sex, but I'm afraid I might get pregnant. I'm too embarrassed to talk to him about birth control and I'm scared to go to a doctor. Is there any way I can use birth control without him knowing about it?"

One reply might be: "What is more important than using a confidential method of birth control is how you feel about sex and birth control. If you are too embarrassed to talk to your boyfriend about it, you need to think long and hard about whether or not you are *deep* down really ready to be sexually involved with him. Having reservations may mean you aren't ready to have an intimate physical relationship with him even though you care about him a great deal. Maybe you sense he isn't mature enough to handle the responsibility of using contraception. Having sex now might not be the right time in your stage of life or in your relationship. If you decide to have a sexual relationship with him, call a county health department, a city family planning clinic, or Planned Parenthood. Whatever you do, don't let your confusion or embarrassment set you up to take the risk of getting pregnant. It's not worth it."

Chapter Ten: The Prospect of Pregnancy

Q. How do you know if you are pregnant?

A. Usually, a sign of pregnancy is missing a period. But that doesn't mean that if you miss a period you are pregnant. Although the first indication is not having your period, other symptoms are swelling of the breasts and "morning sickness," which means you can feel nauseous any time of the day. If a girl is worried about it, she should get a pregnancy test. She could use a home testing kit, but if the directions are not followed very accurately the test could give a false reading (either positive or negative). The most reliable test is a laboratory urinalysis at a clinic, or at a physician's office. The urine is analyzed for a change in the urine's chemicals that indicates pregnancy.

Q. Do "home" pregnancy tests really work?

A. It depends on the test and how accurately the test directions are followed. It is best for a teen to go to a pregnancy testing clinic if she is concerned about being pregnant.

Q. Why do some girls, even though they are having sex and not using anything, not get pregnant?

A. There are probably a lot of reasons. Maybe they had sex during a time they weren't fertile, or the guy's sperm wasn't fertile. But mostly they have been lucky. If they continue to have sex without using contraception, they eventually will become pregnant.

Q. Do you think a couple should get married if the girl gets pregnant?

A. It depends on their ages and their relationship. Some couples have gone together a long time and, although the pregnancy wasn't planned, it might not be unwanted. They could be in good emotional and economical shape and want to marry. But, for teens, I don't think so. Most teens are not emotionally mature enough yet to handle marriage and parenthood. And they usually don't have the financial resources to manage a household of their own. When a teenage couple gets married because of a pregnancy, the marriage almost always doesn't work out. If the girl decides to keep the child, the guy should (and keep in mind that he is legally bound to) provide child support even though they don't marry.

Q. I've heard that guys sometimes deny that they are the father when the girl tells him she is pregnant. Is that very common?

A. Sadly, it is, especially among teenage boys. They are usually in shock, and their first reaction is to try to be absolved of the realities of being involved in a pregnancy—even if they care a lot about the girl. Many guys say they felt "trapped." Flashing before their eyes are the problems of obtaining an abortion, or the emotional turmoil of adoption, or, if she decides to keep the baby, the responsibility ahead. And their reaction, while not laudable, is understandable. They might know, from an experience of someone they know, that becoming a teenage father is no picnic. Here is what some unwed teenage fathers had to say about their problems: "not having enough money to buy clothes and food for the baby"; "she [the teenage mother] wants to get married before I finish school and I want to wait until I get myself straight"; "having a boring job because I had to drop out of school"; and "everything is one big hassle."

Most guys are supportive after the initial shock has worn off, but too often, after the child is a year or so old, many lose interest in being a father because they don't love the girl anymore, they are overwhelmed with trying to go to school or working, or they feel resentful of what fate has dealt them.

Q. How can a guy know for sure if he is the father?

A. If there is any doubt about who is the father of the child, there are blood tests the mother and the alleged father can take. They are about 95 percent accurate. These tests are really more than a simple blood test. They include the human leukocyte group A (HLA) antigen test, which is the most current kind of "paternity" test: an advanced form of tissue typing involving an analysis of matching or unmatching genes of the child, mother, and "father." The older type of blood tests can only prove that a specific male could not be the father because of the incompatibility of his blood group with the child's. For example, usually a person with blood type O doesn't have a child with blood type AB, or vice versa. However, if the man and the mother have had intercourse, and he and the child both have O blood types, the courts may proclaim that man the father of the child, and he could be responsible for child support, even though type O is very common.

Q. Isn't giving up a baby for adoption the hardest thing to do? Even harder than abortion?

A. Neither is easy. Who can say what is more difficult? Many teenage girls who choose adoption feel it is the best thing all around—for them, their baby, and their family. They find solace in knowing that a couple who really wants a baby, and can take good care of a child, will be given such joy by her decision. They may feel they are giving their child the best gift they can—a good family life.

There are two ways a girl can relinquish her baby for adoption: "private" channels through the legal and medical system, and "agencies," which can be private or public. And the arrangements can vary from a closed adoption, in which all of the records are sealed, to an open adoption, where the girl might meet the potential adoptive parents and participate in the placement process. She can choose which type best suits her feelings and hopes for her child.

Q. Does a guy, even if he is a minor and doesn't have a steady job, have to pay out child support?

A. Yes, if he is legally declared the father of the child. Under a recent law, he can be required to help support the child regardless of his age, whether he is married to the child's mother, or if he has a steady job. If he fails to pay, he can be fined by the court, and in some instances serve a jail sentence. Sometimes, a teenage mother is reluctant to name the father of the child, or make him pay child support. However, if an unmarried mother needs to apply to the organization Aid to Families with Dependent Children, and most do, she must declare the father as a condition of eligibility to receive payments. And he, for her to receive these payments, must contribute at least some minimal amount of child support. If he is not legally financially responsible, his parents could be held responsible.

Q. Can a girl get an abortion even if the guy doesn't want her to?
A. Yes. A girl does not need the guy's permission. If she is a minor, she may need her parents' written consent in some cases, but not the guy's.

Q. Can you tell if a girl is not able to get pregnant?
A. Not until she has reached maturity as an adult. If she is not able to get pregnant then (infertile), she can go to an infertility clinic for help. But, for teens, assume she can get pregnant and take steps to protect yourself from an unplanned pregnancy.

Chapter Eleven: A Fact of Life: STDs

Q. How do you know you have the clap?
A. Usually males have a discharge of pus from the penis and a burning feeling when they urinate; females have a yellowish discharge from the vagina. *But* most women have no symptoms at all! And some men don't either. If you think you may have gonorrhea, get tested.

Q. Can you have VD and not know it?
A. Yes, you can, especially gonorrhea, syphilis, or chlamydia.

Q. If you go to a VD clinic, do they tell your parents?
A. No. They won't tell anyone. It is confidential.

Q. Do people still get syphilis?
A. Yes, about 90,000 new cases are reported each year. And the worst part is that many people don't even know they have it.

Q. Is chlamydia the same thing as gonorrhea?
A. They are both sexually transmitted diseases, but chlamydia has both bacterial and viral characteristics. Gonorrhea, however, is only a bacterial infection. Most people (especially women) don't know they have either infection, and both can cause sterility. Usually gonorrhea causes more of a discharge from the penis or the vagina than chlamydia.

Q. If you go to the health clinic, do you have to tell them who you've had sex with?
A. By law, if you have gonorrhea, syphilis, or AIDS, health workers must ask you the names of anyone you have had sex with, but your name is *never* revealed. They have to notify all sexual partners because if these diseases are not treated they may lead to really serious consequences. Health workers are very understanding and only want to safeguard everyone's health.

Q. How can you tell if someone has VD?
A. You can't always tell if someone has a sexually transmitted disease, but you may be able to see some of the symptoms. If you see any kind of sore (blisters, angry-looking pimples) or wart (bumps) around the mouth or genitals of someone, they could be infected. Discharge from the penis or vagina may also be a sign of sexual infection. The best way to know if someone has an STD is to know the person and have an honest relationship with them. If there are

any signs at all of *any* sexual infection, do not have sex with them.

Q. Is it true that if you have herpes, you can't get pregnant?
A. No, having herpes doesn't mean a person can't get pregnant. However, when a pregnant woman has an active case of herpes, the baby shouldn't be delivered vaginally because the disease could present serious complications for the baby.

Q. Can you get VD if you have sex just once?
A. Yes. You get VD from having sex with someone who has a sexually transmitted disease, whether it is the first time or not. The number of times has nothing to do with it. The big problem is that many people who have a sexually transmitted disease don't even know it,

Q. Is it worse to get the clap or worse to get herpes?
A. You really can't say one is worse than the other. The biggest difference is that gonorrhea can be treated and cured with antibiotics, while herpes cannot. On the other hand, genital herpes won't lead to infertility and sterility, whereas gonorrhea, if left untreated, may cause both. It's better not to get either.

REFERENCES

Chapter One: The Way It Is

Belkin, Lisa. "Poll Finds Liberalized Sex View." *New York Times*, May 16, 1985.

Bell, Ruth, and Leni Zeiger Wildflower. *Talking with Your Teen-ager: A Book for Parents*. New York: Random House, 1983.

Burkhart, Kathryn W. "Sex Education Begins in the Home." *Families*, December 1981:113–115.

Lee, Felicia. "Sex Is No Taboo to Teens Today." *USA Today*, May 7, 1985.

Tener, Elizabeth. "Talk to Your Teen-agers about Sex." *Woman's Day*, September 4, 1979 (reprinted in *Reader's Digest*, December 1979).

Chapter Two: Easing into a Discussion

Calderone, Mary, and Eric Johnson. *The Family Book about Sexuality*. New York: Harper and Row, 1981.

Calderone, Mary, and James Ramey. *Talking with Your Child about Sex: Questions and Answers for Children from Birth to Puberty*. New York: Random House, 1982.

Gordon, Sol, and Judith Gordon. *Raising a Child Conservatively in a Sexually Permissive World*. New York: Simon and Schuster, 1983.

Herold, E. "Reasons Given by Female Virgins for Not Having Premarital Intercourse." *Journal of School Health*, September 1981.

Hickler, Holly, and Connie May. "Talking with Adolescents." *The New Voice*, Vol. 1, No. 3. Boston: WGBH-TV, 1984.

Keiffer, Elisabeth. "What Kids Really Want to Know about Sex but Are Afraid to Ask." *Family Circle*, April 17, 1984.

Lewis, Howard R., and Martha E. Lewis. *The Parent's Guide to Teenage Sex and Pregnancy*. New York: St. Martin's Press, 1980.

———. *Sex Education Begins at Home: How to Raise Sexually Healthy Children*. Norwalk, CT: Appleton-Century-Crofts, 1983.

Norman, Jane. *The Private Life of the American Teenager*. New York: Rawson-Wade, 1981.

Pocs, O., and A. Godow. "The Shock of Recognizing Parents as Sexual Beings." In *Exploring Human Sexuality*, edited by D. Byrne and L. Dyrne. New York: Crowell, 1977.

Sorenson, Robert. *Adolescent Sexuality in Contemporary America*. Cleveland: World Publishing Co., 1973.

Chapter Three: Teenagers, aka Adolescents

Bell, Ruth. *Changing Bodies, Changing Lives: A Book for Teens on Sex and Relationships*. New York: Random House, 1980.

Doyle, K. L. L., and Carol Cassell. "Teenage Sexuality: The Early Adolescent Years." In *Obstetrics and Gynecology Annual*, edited by Ralph M. Wynn. New York: Appleton-Century-Crofts, 1981.

Gaddis, Alan, and J. Brooks-Gunn. "The Male Experience of Pubertal Change." *Journal of Youth and Adolescence*, Vol. 14, No. 1, February 1985: 61–69.

Gispert, Maria. "Sexual Conflicts and Concerns of Adolescent Girls." *Medical Aspects of Human Sexuality*, Vol. 50, No. 52 February 1981: 101.

Hunt, Samuel P. "Adolescence and Developmental Aspects of Sexual Orientation." *Medical Aspects of Human Sexuality*, Vol. 14, No. 22, November 1980: 86–88.

Katchadourian, Herant. "The Creation of Adolescence." *Family Life Educator*, Vol. 2, No. 2, Winter 1983: 5–9.

Kelly, Gary. *Learning about Sex: The Contemporary Guide for Young Adults*. New York: Barron Educational Series, 1976.

McCoy, Julie, and Charles Wibbelsman. *The Teenage Body Book*. New York: Simon and Schuster, 1984.

Openshaw, D. Kim, Darwin Thomas, and Boyd Rollins. "Socialization and Adolescent Self-Esteem: Symbolic Interaction and Social Learning Explanations." *Adolescence*, Summer 1983: 316–329.

Ranck, Lee. "Use It Better Than James." *Engage/Social Action*, April 1978:11.

Spain, Julie. *Counseling Adolescents in Reproductive Health Care Settings*. Washington, D.C.: U.S. Department of Health and Human Services, Public Health Service, Bureau of Community Health Service, 1980.

Chapter Four: What Is This Thing Called Love?

Bessell, Harold. "The Love Test." *McCalls*, February 1984.

Cassell, Carol. *Swept Away: Why Women Fear Their Own Sexuality*. New York: Simon and Schuster, 1984.

Gordon, Sol. *How Can You Tell if You're Really in Love?* New York: Ed-U Press, 1983.

Lawrence, D. H. *Lady Chatterley's Lover*. New York: Grove Press Black Cat Edition, 1962, p. 266.

"Love." *Family Life Educator*, Vol. 3, No. 2, Summer 1983.

Masters, William, Virginia Johnson, and Robert Kolodny. *Human Sexuality*. Boston: Little, Brown and Co., 1982. Stanley Schacter quoted on page 236.

May, Rollo. *Love and Will*. New York: W. W. Norton and Co., 1969. Available in trade paperback: New York: Dell Publishing Co., 1973.

O'Neill, Nena, and George O'Neill. *Open Marriage: A New Life Style for Couples*. New York: M. Evans and Co., 1972.

Rosenbaum, Ron. "The Chemistry of Love." *Esquire*, June 1984. Dr. Michael Liebowitz quoted on pages 105–109.

Shope, David. *Interpersonal Sexuality*. Philadelphia: W. B. Saunders Co., 1975, p. 36. Abraham Maslow and Sigmund Freud cited on page 35.

Tennov, Dorothy. *Love and Limerence*. New York: Stein and Day, 1979.

Chapter Five: What Is Sex? I Mean Really!

Adams, Caren, Jennifer Fay, and Jan Loreen-Martin. *No Is Not Enough: Helping Teenagers Avoid Sexual Assault*. San Luis Obispo, CA: Impact Publishers, 1984. The report on teen attitudes about a male forcing a female to have sex is on pages 92–93. Also see "It's Rape," *Family Life Educator*, Vol. 3, No. 1, Fall 1984: 6.

Bell, Ruth, and Leni Zeiger Wildflower. "The Turmoil of Teenage Sexuality: Kids' Coded Messages." *Ms.*, July 1983.

Brody, Jane E. "Guidelines for Parents of Teen-agers Who Are, or Are about to Be, Sexually Active." *New York Times*, Personal Health column, April 30, 1986.

Calderone, Mary Steichen. From a lecture delivered at Vassar College, September 1963.

Chilman, Catherine. *Adolescent Sexuality in a Changing American Society*. New York: John Wiley and Sons, 1983.

Coles, Robert, and Geoffrey Stokes. *Sex and the American Teenager*. New York: Harper and Row/Rolling Stone Press, 1985.

Conaway, James. "Young Conservatives: Stamping Out the '60s." *Washington Post National Weekly Edition*, February 11, 1985. Noreen Barr quoted on page 7.

Diepold, J., Jr., and R. D. Young. "Empirical Studies of Adolescent Sexual Behavior: A Critical Review." *Adolescence*, Vol. 14, No. 53, 1979: 45–64.

Fine, Louis. "Sexual Behavior in Adolescents Has Many Sources." *Albuquerque Journal*, January 16, 1978.

Goodman, Ellen. "The Turmoil of Teenage Sexuality: Parents' Mixed Signals." *Ms.*, July 1983. Elizabeth Roberts and Carol Gilligan quoted on page 40.

Gordon, Sol, Peter Scales, and Kathleen Everly. *The Sexual Adolescent: Communicating with Teenagers about Sex*, 2nd edition. North Scituate, MA: Duxbury Press, 1979.

John, O. G., and Bill and J. Richard Udry. "The Influence of Male and Female Best Friends on Adolescent Sexual Behavior." *Adolescence*, Spring 1985: 21–32.

Kolodny, Robert, Nancy J. Kolodny, Thomas Bratter, and Cheryl Deep. *How to Survive Your Adolescent's Adolescence*. New York: Little, Brown and Co., 1984.

Libby, Roger. "Adolescent Sexual Attitudes and Behavior." *Journal of Clinical Child Psychology*, Vol. III, No. 3, Fall/Winter 1974: 36–43. Although this issue is over ten years old, the information remains relevant.

Masters, William, Virginia Johnson, and Robert Kolodny. *Human Sexuality*. Boston: Little, Brown and Co., 1982.

Mayle, Peter. "*Will I Like It?*" New York: Corwin Books, 1977. Not for the faint-at-heart parent as it describes first intercourse for teens and how to make it more satisfying.

Nelson, Emily. "Responsible Sexuality." *Impact*, 1979.

Newcomer, Susan, and J. Richard Udry. "Parent-Child Communication and Adolescent Sexual Behavior." *Family Planning Perspectives*, Vol. 17, No. 4, July/August 1985:169–175.

Nonkin, Lesley Jane. *I Wish My Parents Understood*. New York: Penguin Books, 1985.

Philliber, Susan G., and Mary Lee Tatum. "Sex Education and the Double Standard in High School." *Adolescence*, Vol. 17, No. 66, Summer 1982:273–283.

Pogrebin, Letty Cottin. *Growing Up Free: Raising Your Child in the '80s*. New York: McGraw-Hill, 1980. The quote on male sexual rules is on page 271.

Sorenson, Robert. "Adolescent Sexuality: Crucible for Generational Conflict." *Journal of Clinical Child Psychology*, Vol. III, No. 3, Fall/Winter 1974:44–47.

"Teenagers and Sex: The Price of Freedom." *Families*, Vol. 1, No. 2, May 1981 (reprinted from *Newsweek*, September 1, 1980).

"Teens Are More Sexually Active." *Washington Post*, May 18, 1985.

Towarnicky, Carol. "For Teenage Girls, Life Still Is Not Much Fun." *Daily News*, May 12, 1985. A good review of Lesley Jane Nonkin's study.

Van Buren, Abigail. "What Every Teenager Ought to Know." A *Dear Abby* booklet, 1979. Available from Abigail van Buren, P.O. Box 38923, Hollywood, CA 90038.

Zabin, Laurie, Marilyn Hirsch, Edward Smith, and Janet Hardy. "Adolescent Sexual Attitudes and Behavior: Are They Consistent?" *Family Planning Perspectives*, Vol. 16, No. 4, July/August 1984:181–185.

Zelnik, Melvin, and Farida Shah. "First Intercourse among Young Americans." *Family Planning Perspectives*, Vol. 15, No. 2, March/April 1983:64–69.

Chapter Six: Relationships and Such

Adams, Caren, et al. *No Is Not Enough: Helping Teenagers Avoid Sexual Assault*. San Luis Obispo, CA: Impact Publishers, 1984. Chapter 7, "Just Friends: Overcoming Sex Role Expectations," discusses sex-role stereotyping and the need for male-female friendships.

Eagan, Andrea Boroff. *Why Am I So Miserable if These Are the Best Years of My Life?* New York: Avon, 1979.

"Expectations Not Sexual Development Influence Adolescent Dating Behavior." *Sexuality Today*, June 8, 1981. Sandford Dornbusch is quoted on pages 2–3.

Hass, Aaron. *Teenage Sexuality: A Survey of Teenage Sexual Behavior*. New York: Macmillan, 1979.

Lindsay, Jeanne Warren. *Teens Look at Marriage: Rainbows, Roles and Reality*. Buena Park, CA: Morning Glory Press, 1985.

Miles, Herbert. *The Dating Game*. Grand Rapids, MI: Zondervan Publishing House, 1977. David Mace is quoted on page 33.

Montemayor, Raymond, and Roger Van Komen. "The Development of Sex Differences in Friendship Patterns and Peer Group Structure during Adolescence." *Journal of Early Adolescence*, Vol. 5, No. 3, Fall 1985: 285–294.

Moore, Kristin, Sandra Hofferth, Steven Caldwell, and Linda Waite. *Teenage Motherhood: Social and Economic Consequences*. Washington, D.C.: The Washington Urban Institute, 1979.

Pietropinto, Anthony. "Adolescent Dating." *Medical Aspects of Human Sexuality*, Vol. 18, No. 12, December 1984: 113ff.

Pogrebin, Letty Cottin. *Growing Up Free: Raising Your Child in the '80s*. New York: McGraw-Hill, 1980. Chapter 5, "Friendship and Fun," is one of the best I've seen on the importance of friendship for young people.

Roscoe, Bruce, and John Callahan. "Adolescent's Self-Report of Violence in Families and Dating Relations." *Adolescence*, Vol. 20, No. 79, Fall 1985: 545–553.

Rosemond, John. "Adolescence Sometimes Yells 'Boo.' " *Albuquerque Journal*, September 14, 1985.

Rubin, Lillian. *Just Friends: The Role of Friendship in Our Lives*. New York: Harper and Row, 1985.

Scales, Cynthia, and Peter Scales. "Dating Dilemmas." *Current Health and Current Lifestudies*, Supplement, Vol. 9, No. 2, October 1982.

Schowalter, John, and Walter Anyan, Jr. *The Family Handbook of Adolescence*. New York: Alfred A. Knopf, 1979.

Sofferin, Pam, et al. "Life Styles." *Education and Counseling Program*, Pensacola, Fla.: Child Development Service, 1984.

Spreadbury, Connie. "First Date." *Journal of Early Adolescence*, Vol. 2, No. 1, Spring 1982: 83–89.

"What 100 Teenagers Think about Dating." *Co-Ed Magazine*, November 1984.

Chapter Seven: Surviving a Broken Heart

Colgrove, Melba, Harold Bloomfield, and Peter McWilliams. *How to Survive the Loss of a Love*. New York: Leo Press, 1976. Available in trade paperback: New York: Bantam, 1983.

Masters, William, Virginia Johnson, and Robert Kolodny. *Human Sexuality*. Studies on college-age students are cited on page 233.

Mazur, Carol. "Alas, All Things Must Pass." *Albuquerque Journal*, July 7, 1985: 1.

Whitman, Ardis. "When Someone You Love Leaves You." *Woman's Day*, April 6, 1982.

Winship, Elizabeth. *Ask Beth, You Can't Ask Your Mother*. Boston: Houghton Mifflin Co., 1976. Also, look for her syndicated column "Ask Beth"—it's full of good advice for teens and almost-teens.

Chapter Eight: Homosexuality/Homophobia

"Gallup Poll Survey: Americans' Attitudes toward Gays." *Family Life Educator*, Vol. 2, No. 1, Fall 1983: 27.

Gordon, Sol, and Judith Gordon. *Raising a Child Conservatively in a Sexually Permissive World*. New York: Simon and Schuster, 1983, p. 136. Also check their index for more information on homosexuality.

"Growing Up Gay." *Newsweek*, January 13, 1986. The quote from Wayne Pawlowski is cited on page 50. Rita Mae Brown and Joyce Hunter are quoted on page 52.

Lewis, Howard R. and Martha E. Lewis. *Sex Education Begins at Home*. Norwalk, CT: Appleton-Century-Crofts, 1983. See Chapter 11, "Same-Sex Contacts." Grace and Fred Hechinger's study and quote are from Dr. Thomas Merrifield and are cited on page 163. The quote from Alfred Kinsey is on page 166 and his teenage studies are reported on page 153. The quote from Evelyn Hooker is on page 173. Lester Kirkendall's study is cited on page 152.

Marmor, Judd (ed.). *Homosexual Behavior*. New York: Basic Books, 1980.

Masters, William, Virginia Johnson, and Robert Kolodny. *Human Sexuality*. Boston: Little, Brown, and Co., 1982. See Chapter 13, "Homosexuality and Bisexuality." Information on Alfred Kinsey's studies is on page 316. The Alan Bell and Martin Weinberg studies are cited on page 330.

Pogrebin, Letty Cottin. *Growing Up Free: Raising Your Child in the '80s*. New York: McGraw-Hill, 1980. See Chapter 15, "Homosexuality, Hysteria and Children: How Not to Be a Homophobic Parent." The studies on social and psychological adjustment are cited on page 286.

Reiss, B. F. "Psychological Tests in Homosexuality." In *Homosexual Behavior*, edited by J. Marmor. New York: Basic Books, 1980, pp. 296–311.

Chapter Nine: Hmmm, What about Contraception?

Bachrach, Christine. "Contraceptive Practice among American Women, 1973–1982." *Family Planning Perspectives*, Vol. 16, No. 6, November/December 1984: 253–259.

Bingham, Maren. "Sex Education: Majority Favor Its Place in School but a Vocal Minority Thwart Effort." *Arizona Republic*, July 21, 1985.

Cassell, Carol. "A Perspective on the Great Sex Education Debate." In *Challenges in Sexual Science: Current Theoretical Issues and Research Advances*, edited by Clive Davis. Lake Mills, IA: Graphic Publishing Co., 1983.

———. "The Politics of Sex Education: Campaigns and Crusades." In *Adolescent Reproductive Health*, edited by Peggy Smith and David Mumford. New York: Gardner Press, 1985.

Chng, Chwee Lye. "The Male Role in Contraception: Implications for Health Education." *Journal of School Health*, Vol. 53, No. 3, March 1983: 197–201.

Goodman, Ellen. "Her Kinkiest Media Fantasies for 1985." *Albuquerque Journal*, March 19, 1985.

Jones, Elise, Jacqueline Forrest, Noreen Goldman, Stanley Henshaw, Richard Lincoln, Jeannie Rosoff, Charles Westoff, and Deirdre Wulf. "Teenage Pregnancy in Developed Countries: Determinants and Policy Implications." *Family Planning Perspectives*, Vol. 17, No. 2, March/April 1985: 53–63.

Kisker, Ellen. "Teenagers Talk about Sex, Pregnancy and Contraception." *Family Planning Perspectives*, Vol. 17, No. 2, March/April 1985: 83–90.

Mann, Judy. "Hypocrisy in Prime Time." *Washington Post*, July 6, 1985.

McLellan, Elizabeth (ed.). *The Patient Patients' Book*. Ithaca, NY: Challenge Industries, 1980.

Ory, Howard, and Jacqueline Forrest. *Making Choices: Evaluating the Health Risks and Benefits of Birth Control Methods*. New York: Alan Guttmacher Institute, 1983.

Polit-O'Hara and Janet Kahn. "Communication and Contraceptive Practices in Adolescent Couples." *Adolescence*, Spring 1985: 33–43.

Richards, Arlene, and Irene Willis. "Teenager's Guide to Sex Safety." *Ms.*, July 1983.

Stewart, Felicia, Gary Stewart, Felicia Guest, and Robert Hatcher. *My Body, My Health*. New York: John Wiley and Sons, 1985.

Chapter Ten: The Prospect of Pregnancy

Auletta, Ken. "Children of Children." *Parade Magazine*, June 17, 1984. See statistics on teenage pregnancy and teen abortion and adoption rates.

Booth, Alan, and John Edwards. "Age at Marriage and Marital Instability." *Journal of Marriage and the Family*, Vol. 47, No. 1, February 1985:67–75.

"Children Having Children," *Time*, December 9, 1985. See statistics on out-of-wedlock pregnancies.

"Contraception Is Less Risky for Teenagers than Is Pregnancy." *Family Planning Perspectives*, Vol. 14, No. 5, September/October 1982: 274–276.

"Facts You Should Know about Teenage Pregnancy." *March of Dimes*, October 1984.

McClelland, Eileen. "Teen Mothers Share Feelings about Pregnancy." *Columbiana County, Morning Journal*, July 10, 1984.

Patten, Marie. "Self-Concept and Self-Esteem: Factors in Adolescent Pregnancy." *Adolescence*, Winter 1981: 765–778.

"Preliminary Findings Released on First Study of 12–15-Year-Old Mothers." Washington, D.C.: Child Welfare League of America, new release, 1982.

Rosen, Raye, Twylah Benson, and Jack Stack. "Help or Hindrance: Parental Impact on Pregnant Teenagers' Resolution Decisions." *Family Relations*, Vol. 30, No. 2, April 1981: 271–280.

Steere, Mike. "Teen-Age Parents Tell Their Stories." *The Toledo Blade*, March 23, 1981.

"U.S. Leads Developed Nations in Rate of Teen-age Pregnancy." *Education Week*, March 20, 1985.

Yancey, Dwayne. "Series on Teenage Pregnancy." *Roanoke Times and World News*, August 3–6, 1985.

Chapter Eleven: A Fact of Life: STDs

"AIDS Forcing Gays to Alter Habits." *Albuquerque Tribune*, May 19, 1986, p. B-1.

"AIDS: What Are the Facts?" *Oregon Department of Human Resources*, November 1985.

Lumiere, Richard, and Stephani Cook. *Healthy Sex: And Keeping It That Way: A Complete Guide to Sexual Infections*. New York: Simon and Schuster, 1983.

McCoy, Kathy, and Charles Wibbelsman. *The Teenage Body Book*. New York: A Wallaby Book, Simon and Schuster, 1984.

"A Nasty New Epidemic." *Newsweek*, February 4, 1985.

Tanne Hopkins, Janice. "AIDS: Is Anyone Safe?" *Reader's Digest*, February 1986. The quote of Dr. Helen Singer Kaplan is on page 64.

"What Do We Know about AIDS—1985 Update." *Family Life Educator*, Vol. 4, No. 1, Fall 1985.

Withington, Amelia, David Grimes, and Robert Hatcher. *Teenage Sexual Health*. New York: Irvington Publishers, Inc., 1983.

SELECTED RESOURCES

There are any number of really good resources for your teen about sexuality; those I've listed here are only a few I like the best. I probably forgot some, so be sure and check with your local library, especially with the librarian who specializes in books for young people and can make suggestions for material that will suit your teenager.

I've also listed some resources for you that talk about adolescence in general, or that deal with a specific area in more detail than I covered.

FOR TEENS

Bell, Ruth, et al. *Changing Bodies, Changing Lives.* New York: Random House, 1981. Talks to teens about facts and feelings about sex and relationships. It also shares with teens other teenagers' opinions and experiences.

Betancourt, Jeanne. *Am I Normal?* and *Dear Diary*. New York: Avon Books, 1983. Deals with emotional and physical changes of puberty for boys and girls, respectively.

All of Judy Blume's books. She is young people's favorite author; she is insightful and honest about teenagers' feelings and experiences. I particularly like *Forever* (New York: Pocket Books, 1984). Just go to your bookstore and ask to see Judy Blume's books for young people. You can go to the library but they can't keep her books on the shelves.

Changes: You and Your Body. A nifty little pamphlet. Available from Choice, 1501 Cherry St., Philadelphia, PA 19102.

Comfort, Alex, and Jane Comfort. *The Facts of Love: Living, Loving and Growing Up*. New York: Crown Publishers, 1979. A dynamic book about sexuality, ideal as an ice-breaker for conversation with your teen.

Eagan, A. B. *Why Am I So Miserable if These Are the Best Years of My Life?* New York: Avon, 1979. She talks to girls in a very understanding voice, and gives them some practical advice.

Gordon, Sol. He has the knack of giving kids solid information without boring them into a deep sleep. A very important book for teens is *The Teenage Survival Book* (New York: Times Books, 1981). It has lists for teens to fill out and gives them brief pieces of wisdom to think about. His other books include *Facts about Sex for Today's Youth* and *Facts about STDs* (New York: Ed-U Press, 1983). These are great for teens who don't like to read much. Also, his book *You Would if You Loved Me* (New York: Bantam Books, 1974) is perfect for teens who need a little help on how *not* to give and fall for "lines."

Johnson, Eric. *Love and Sex in Plain Language*, 4th ed., New York: Harper and Row, 1985. This is a gem. It provides basic information on sexuality, and emphasizes that sexuality should be seen in the context of one's total personality and expressed in responsible, respectful interpersonal relationships.

Kelly, Gary. *Learning about Sex: The Contemporary Guide for Young Adults.* New York: Barron's Educational Series, 1977. Besides the basic facts, he talks about the process of decision making and focuses on sexual values.

Loulan-Gardner, JoAnn, et al. *Period.* San Francisco: Volcano Press, 1979. A reassuring illustrated book about menstruation.

Mayle, Peter. *What's Happening to Me?* New York: Lyle Stuart, Inc., 1975. A funny, clear, and concise guide to the wonders of puberty for pre-adolescents.

McNaught, Brian. *A Disturbed Peace.* Washington, D.C.: Dignity Publications, 1981. A wonderfully touching and witty book about growing up gay. Also, order his candid video presentation, *On Being Gay* (TRB Productions, P.O. Box 2362, Boston, MA 02107). Brian talks about the facts and the feelings of being gay in a straight world, and he encourages both gay and non-gay viewers to realize their own potential and replace self-hate with self-esteem. I think this is helpful to all teens (and adults) no matter their sexual orientation.

The Pregnant Male. This pamphlet talks about the role of men in deciding the future of a pregnancy, including what happens during and after abortion. From Midwest Health Center for Women, 825 South 8th St., Minneapolis, MN 55404.

Rosenberg, Ellen. *Growing Up, Feeling Good.* New York: Beaufort Books, Inc., 1983. An upbeat book for preadolescents about everything they are concerned about. It's also good for parents.

Westheimer, Ruth. *First Love.* New York: Warner Books, 1985. A good book that talks about young people's feelings and covers the facts of life. Because most kids know who she is and watch her TV show, they would be receptive to reading it.

Also, here are some places you might want to write for their material:

Channing Bete publishes scriptographic booklets on a variety of topics for young people: Channing L. Bete Co., South Deerfield, MA 01373.

The Family Life Education Publishing Cooperative, ETR Associates, 1700 Mission St., Suite 203, P.O. Box 1830, Santa Cruz, CA 95061-1830. Ask about their catalog, it is chock full of current books and pamphlets about all areas of sexuality. Also, it has several of the pamphlets I have listed.

Check with your local Planned Parenthood to see what they have available for sale, or for loan from their library. And you can write to the national office: Planned Parenthood Federation of America Publications, 810 Seventh Avenue, New York, NY 10019.

RAJ Publications, P.O. Box 18599, Denver, CO 80218. These publications don't waffle around; they are straightforward, and kids like them. Especially inquire about *The Perils of Puberty* and *The Problem with Puberty*.

FOR YOU

Adams, Caren, et al. *No Is Not Enough: Helping Teens Avoid Sexual Assault*. San Luis Obispo, CA: Impact Publishers, 1984. Helps parents in talking with teenagers about sexual assault and provides guides on how parents can help protect teenagers from sexual assault and exploitation. A must reading.

Blume, Judy. *Letters to Judy: What Your Kids Wish They Could Tell You.* New York: G. P. Putnam's Sons, 1986. A peek inside what is on kids' minds along with comments from Judy about her own coming-of-age experiences. It will inspire all parents to start communicating better with their kids.

Calderone, Mary, and James Ramey. *Talking with Your Child about Sex.* New York: Random House, 1982. Easy to read, for those of you who have young children.

Carrera, Michael. *Sex: The Facts, the Acts, and Your Feelings.* New York: Crown, 1981. An encyclopedia of sexuality. This is a good book for mature teenagers, too.

Fairchild, Betty, and Nancy Hayward. *Now That You Know: What Every Parent Should Know about Homosexuality.* New York: Harcourt Brace Jovanovich, 1984. A primer for parents by the mother of a lesbian and the mother of a gay man.

Hite, Shere. *The Hite Report: A Nationwide Study of Family Sexuality.* New York: Dell Books, 1977.

Hite, Shere. *The Hite Report of Male Sexuality.* New York: Ballantine Books, 1981.

Kolodny, Robert, et al. *How to Survive Your Adolescent's Adolescence.* New York: Little, Brown and Co., 1984. An essential book for your library. It covers everything about adolescence you need to know.

McIlvenna, Ted, Ph.D., ed. *The Complete Guide to Safe Sex.* Beverly Hills, CA: The Specific Press, 1987. Published by the Institute for Advanced Study of Human Sexuality.

Nonkin, Lesley Jane. *I Wish My Parents Understood.* New York: Penguin Books, 1985. A very eye-opening book about a survey Nonkin conducted among teenage girls to find out what they think about sex, status, education, marriage, and, of course, boys. A terrific way to understand the world of teenage girls. Warning: It is guaranteed to jolt the complacency out of card-carrying feminists.

Pogrebin, Letty Cottin. *Growing Up Free: Raising Your Child in the '80s*. New York: McGraw-Hill, 1980. The very best book for helping you eliminate sex-role stereotyping in your teen's life. This should be given to *every* parent before their child is born. Although it wasn't available when my kids were young, it has been invaluable to me as my teens mature into adults, and in my work with teenagers. Buy it.

For health care for your teen, contact The Society for Adolescent Medicine, P.O. Box 8462, Granada Hills, CA 91344. They can refer parents to doctors and clinics throughout the country that specialize in adolescent health care. Send them a legal-size, stamped, self-addressed envelope.

The best all-round book on sexually transmitted diseases is *Healthy Sex: And Keeping It That Way* by Richard Lumiere, M.D., and Stephani Cook (New York: Simon and Schuster, 1983). It has technical information, but is easy to read. Read it first, then discuss it with your teen. Next, give it to them to keep.

For the VD National Hotline: 1-800-227-8922; 1-800-982-5883 in California.

AND AT LAST

Treat yourself. Get Delia Ephron's book *Teenage Romance: Or How to Die of Embarrassment* (New York: Viking Press, 1981). It's a great laugh.

ABOUT THE AUTHOR

Carol Cassell, Ph.D., is a nationally recognized leader in the field of sexuality education. She is a former president of the American Association of Sex Educators, Counselors and Therapists, a recipient of the Institute of Family Research and Education's Margaret Sanger Award, and was the first director of Planned Parenthood Federation of America, Department of Education.

Dr. Cassell has been featured on numerous television programs including The Phil Donahue Show, The Today Show, and Hour Magazine to name a few. Articles about her research have appeared in *The New York Times*, *McCalls*, and *Glamour.* She is a consulting editor to *The Journal of Sex Education and Therapy*.